\* \* \*

# KNOCKOUT

*To Marieli,*

*Thank you for*
*supporting this book*
*about a So. Bx*
*untold story.*

*Julio Pr*
*8/17*

* * *

# KNOCKOUT

*Fidel Castro Visits The South Bronx*

JULIO PABÓN

ISBN: 0692725512
ISBN 13: 9780692725511

# FORWARD

*"Las palabras no caen en el vacío."*

<u>Zohar</u>

*"Words (written) do not fall into the void."*

Quote from the prologue to <u>El siglo de las luces</u>
by Cuban novelist Alejo Crapentier, one of Latin
America's foremost 20th century writers.

In this short memoir, Julio Pabón offers an extremely detailed and personal, and necessarily subjective reminiscence of the persons involved and preparations leading up to the historical, yet not well remembered visit by Fidel Castro to the Bronx in 1995, and the sense of community pride and personal accomplishment in pulling off what many thought would be highly unlikely or even impossible to carry out.

1995 was a special year for the United Nations since it marked the 50th anniversary of its founding. World leaders met as usual in October but special celebratory events were organized for the occasion, among them a dinner hosted by the Mayor of NYC. When (then) Mayor Rudolph Giuliani realized somewhat belatedly that his guest list included individuals whom he detested for personal as well as political reasons, such as PLO leader Yasser Arafat and Cuba's president Fidel Castro, he issued a press release revoking their invitation.

It was no secret at that time that the bulk of the Mayor's political support came from boroughs other than the Bronx with its large number of Puerto Rican residents. To many, this action by the Mayor appeared to be yet another indication of disdain for the Hispanic population of the borough and New York City as well as an opportunity by the Mayor to embarrass political rivals.

As one of the self-styled "atrevidos" or daring activists, Pabón and several of his close friends and acquaintances felt a need to respond to Giuliani's disrespect of the Bronx and the Hispanic community in general by issuing and alternative invitation to Castro to visit the Bronx. It would be a way to draw attention to an area of the city they perceived to be, at the very least, completely neglected by the Mayor's administration and, at most, punished for its majority of Democratic-leaning residents. Pabón reasoned, what would other Hispanic communities think of the residents of the Bronx if they did nothing in the face of this affront? To assist him, he enlisted the help of key partners, among them Carlos Nazario, President of the National Puerto Rican Business Council to Congressman José E. Serrano.

What started as a brief visit to the Bronx for an intimate dinner for Castro and a selected group of Latinos, however, turned out to be much more complicated and consequential than originally imagined. Pabón arranged for a well-known Bronx location by convincing the owner of Jimmy's Bronx Café to host the event and benefit from the extensive publicity it would receive from the news media. In a span of two days, the dinner expanded from 25 guests to a gathering of 300. Additional complications involved coordinating the agenda, guest list and the logistics with dubious and reluctantly helpful U.S. Secret Service agents and their Cuban counterparts, who were fearful of potential assassination attempts on the guest of honor. Pabón provides us with a list of unexpected fires to be extinguished at every point in the process, including outside demonstrators (supporters of Castro as well anti-Castro protesters who, according to the author, had been paid by the conservative Cuban American National Foundation). He strongly suspects that the cancelation of his radio program by a local station following the event was directly connected to his participation in organizing the dinner, and he adds it to his list of personal sacrifices made to bring the event to fruition.

As one of the invitees that evening, I had only scant notion at the time of the many hurdles that had to be cleared in preparation for this event which was, in the final analysis, smoothly and professionally executed. Introductory comments made by the organizers, who did not raise any controversial issues such as human rights violations, allowed the guest of honor to wax eloquent on what he considered the major achievements of the Cuban Revolution. As expected, in the home of the Yankees, he also spoke about baseball, and touched on a number of non-political topics. Castro's speech was uncharacteristically brief, and the audience was surprisingly respectful even though many in attendance were not supportive of the Castro regime, which they viewed as a dictatorship. Questions and comments from the audience were not allowed and, after Mr. Castro's address, the event ended quietly.

Thinking about Mr. Castro's historic visit to the Bronx more than two decades later, I cannot imagine such an event happening now and, event if it did, that it would be carried out with such civility. In a post 9/11 world, in which terrorist attacks have become commonplace around the world, safety concerns would make it impossible for a controversial figure like Castro to venture to locations and buildings that cannot be easily secured. Further complicating matters, today's ubiquitous social media magnifies every slight and invites multiple dangers from every corner. Whether invited or not, users – thousands or millions of them-comment on events in real time, often with accompanying images and sounds. In a matter of minutes, crowds are able to gather to protest, making it difficult, in not impossible, for law enforcement agencies to respond appropriately to prevent tragic situations from occurring.

In October 1995, Pabón had a unique opportunity, and he did not let it pass him by. Drawing upon his organizational skills as a full-throated advocate for the borough and for the Puerto Rican/Hispanic community, with the assistance of key friends and allies, this "atrevido" achieved something no one else had done before. In honoring Fidel Castro at a dinner, he simultaneously challenged a major that nay fellow Bronxites felt had insulted the people of Cuba and the broader NY and the US Hispanic community and projected a positive light on his home borough.

Were it not for this small book, a memorable chapter in the development of the Puerto Rican and Hispanic community of New York City might be lost to future generations. As the president of Lehman College, the senior college of the City University of New York in the Bronx, I find it most fitting that one of our graduates is the book's author. I extend congratulations and best wishes to him and his partners for bringing to light a unique event in the history of our community.

Ricardo R. Fernández, Ph.D.
Bronx, New York
July 2016

\* \* \*

# DEDICATION

I dedicate this book to my father, Julio Pabón Rivera, who raised me as a single parent; from the time I was 9 years old. He was 50, when I was born. Like countless others from Puerto Rico, he came to New York in search of better opportunities. He came to work on the farms in upstate New York and in Long Island, where he quickly learned that the promises made in Puerto Rico about great paying jobs and opportunities were all lies. My father was a U.S. citizen who was always treated as an immigrant because of his dark complexion and because he did not speak English. He was old enough to be my grandfather. However, his age was a blessing because although we missed sharing many physical activities like playing catch, or football, or going to the movies, the wisdom and knowledge that he engendered in me, provided the foundation for my survival and existence. I was able to survive the worst of the South Bronx because he taught me the importance of making intelligent decisions. He made me understand the importance of learning every day. Each night before going to bed he would ask me, "*¿que tu aprendiste hoy?*" (What did you learn today?). He would make me think and if I took a long time in answering, he would tell me how important it was to learn something every day. He would stress to me that if a day went by that I did not learn anything, it was a wasted day and I could not afford to waste any days. He also taught me to stand up for what I believe in no matter the consequences, and to be "*un hombre de palabra,*" (a man of his word) and to believe that nothing is impossible as long as you have God in your heart. I am who I am today because of his love and his guidance.

# TABLE OF CONTENTS

# PREFACE

In 1995, Cuba's President Fidel Castro visited the South Bronx. Never has a visit by a foreign dignitary caused such a stir in a community that rarely received anything but negative news coverage. Although Castro's visit was widely covered by the traditional corporate media, few people know the story behind his visit. This book tells how an idea on how a response to a mayor's insult resulted in the most famous visit of a Latin American leader to the heart of a Latino community in the United States that was undergoing its own revolution.

Over the years, I have shared anecdotes about that dinner in gatherings with family and friends. Almost every time I told a bit of the story of Fidel's visit, people would tell me that I should write about it. Finally in 2014, I decided to do that and begin writing this story to share with the world.

# INTRODUCTION

Fidel Castro's visit to the Bronx in 1995 was historic for many reasons. For one, it showed the power of a community that many thought was dormant. During the 1990s, Puerto Ricans, specifically in the Bronx, were struggling with some of the worst living conditions in the city, if not the nation. We were a community trying to recuperate from almost two decades of some of the worst intentional destruction of housing structures in the U.S. and the worst quality of life the borough had ever experienced. I witnessed how greedy landlords learned to make bigger profits by denying services for the upkeep of their buildings. It was principally African-Americans and growing numbers of Latinos, the majority of who were Puerto Ricans, who occupied the buildings. Greed led to fast profit when the buildings were torched to collect insurance money, or to instant relief from debt for landlords who simply abandoned their properties.[i]

By 1995, the population of the Bronx was 48 percent Latino, with close to a quarter of a million Puerto Ricans. The borough should have been the Mecca of the Puerto Rican community in the mainland U.S., since it had more Puerto Rican residents than most towns in Puerto Rico. The Bronx had more Puerto Rican elected officials than any other borough and more than any state in the country. Puerto Rican culture was so prevalent that one of the borough's nicknames was and still is, *"El Condado de la Salsa"* (the borough of Salsa music). Despite its potential, our community was still one of the poorest and most neglected in the city. The South Bronx was rated 40th among 42 neighborhoods in New York City on quality of life indicators. Approximately 33 percent of all the households in the community were headed by a single female parent.[ii] Pressures continued to mount: At that point in time, The Metropolitan Transit Authority had raised the price of a public transportation token by 25 cents, despite citywide protest. Tuition at the public City University of New York (CUNY) was also increased, despite citywide student demonstrations against the move.

Though police brutality was rampant throughout the city, tensions were the highest in the Bronx, especially after the police killing of Anthony Baez, a young Puerto Rican who died when a police officer placed him in a choke hold after an argument with police when his football hit a police car. Baez, who suffered from asthma, died from asphyxiation. His killer, police officer Francis Livoti, who had 11 previous accusations of brutality, was exonerated on the charge of homicide when the court decided there was a "technical error" in the indictment. Frequent protests in response to the court's decision forced Bronx District Attorney, Robert Johnson to convene a grand jury in October 1995 in connection with Baez' death, several days before Castro's visit to the South Bronx. Communities of color in the city were constantly at odds with Mayor Rudolph Giuliani, who was widely viewed as insensitive to their needs.

The South Bronx in October 1995 had many of the conditions of a Third World country. Those conditions fostered an environment that made it easy for so many, including myself, to look favorably on the idea of inviting President Castro to visit, especially after Mayor Giuliani disinvited him to a dinner of world leaders he was offering. So what was I thinking at the time? Perhaps President Castro knew about the South Bronx? There was also the fact that I was raised to believe that everything happens for a reason. Perhaps the universe planned for President Castro to visit a borough that indeed had the conditions for change. That would make a visit from a person who led a historic change not only in Cuba, but also in the political landscape of Latin America and Africa, occur against all odds. Perhaps President Castro was the right person to visit and provide hope to a community in need of believing that nothing is impossible. Yet, as historic as President Fidel Castro's visit was to our borough, the event has been forgotten. The few that do remember it are unaware of the circumstances that allowed that visit to take place.

Personally, I love history. My bachelor's degree was in American history and after graduation my first job was as a social studies teacher in the same junior high school that I attended, JHS 38 on St. Ann's Avenue in the Bronx. I love reading and learning from past experiences. Therefore, looking back to those incredible few days of October 1995 and reflecting on how that historic dinner with Fidel Castro took place, has forced me to practice a primary lesson of history: document it, learn from it, and don't let it be forgotten.

I am proud of my role in bringing about that historic encounter. Today, more than twenty years later, I write this from personal experience --- the experience of an individual, a Puerto Rican, who loves his *Condado De La Salsa*, his *Boogie Down Bronx*, and who wants to share a piece of Bronx Borough history that should never be forgotten. The lessons learned were many. I hope this inspires others to pursue ideas to an end, to work with others tirelessly and respectfully, and to recognize that in unity there is strength!

# WHAT PREPARED ME FOR THE IDEA TO INVITE PRESIDENT FIDEL CASTRO?

My community commitment started in my early teens when I began working with organizations like Justicia Latina, the Young Lords Party and El Comité – MINP (*Movimiento de Izquierda Nacional Puertorriqueño*), which helped forge the rebelliousness in me to always challenge the status quo.

After those years I went through a major political transformation, moving from an involvement with extreme left politics, into the mainstream of electoral politics. It started in my last year of undergraduate school at Lehman College when I was president of Frente Unido Latino, the first Latino political club on campus. Latinos were a small minority on campus and to get any resources for the club I had to deal with the school administration and the multicultural student government. Those experiences of negotiating to get what we needed for our club, planted the seeds that prepared me for my eventual jobs working for the Recruitment & Training Program (RTP), a national organization funded by the Department of Labor and responsible for getting African Americans, Latinos and woman into the hard to get into construction trade unions; Avco RTP Joint Venture responsible for operating the South Bronx Job Corps and eventually working for elected officials.

Assemblyman José Serrano was the first and only elected official with whom I had any contact during my radical days. Serrano was a young, newly elected Assemblyman in the South Bronx who wanted to learn about his community beyond his own experience growing up in the Millbrook Projects and working for the South Bronx Community Corporation. During my last years in Lehman College, I would organize some wild parties in my apartment on Cauldwell Avenue, where I lived with two other upperclassmen, Victor Quintana and Humberto Rosado. Assemblyman Serrano was always invited to our wild and popular parties. He would come and make a cameo appearance.

That building became the organizing center of the block. We were three Puerto Rican college students living in the heart of the South Bronx in a ghetto building where few had graduated from high school. As a result we turned that building into the "happening" building on the block. We kept the building clean, and the junkies and thieves respected the fact that we were always helping out and protecting the community from incidents of police brutality and landlord abuses. We became the community social service hub where neighbors would come and ask for our help — everything from translating a letter into Spanish that they had received in English; to helping them fill out government forms for some kind of assistance. We were always available for whatever they needed. I remember, for example, that once we served as the impromptu *congueros* (conga players) for a *Santero* feast (Feast for Saints) held in someone's apartment. Since we controlled three apartments, when any one of us had a party it was as if the whole building plus the three of us had a party, with something happening in every apartment that we controlled. Thus it was safe for anyone to attend as we compartmentalized each one.

One apartment was where the weed was smoked and where the less important political conversations and debates took place. Another apartment was where all the lovers who could not wait to get home would congregate. My apartment was the largest; I had three bedrooms because I was the only student with children. My apartment was a "no drug zone" and thus would be the place for families to mingle, where revolutionaries and sympathizers could have political discussions, and the main place for pure unadulterated music and dancing. I had the best sound system and the best salsa. It was also the "safe" apartment to visit, and it was there that José Serrano and some of our college professors, intellectuals, and artists would mingle and perform, with many others coming in and out of the parties from the other apartments.

In those early days, I was learning the art of dealing with everyone without judging anyone. Those experiences taught this hardcore South Bronx kid, raised in poverty by a single parent, who should have been a negative statistic, to survive in the cement jungle of New York City. I was slowly moving out of politics, both electoral, and to some degree, leftist political activism. I was concentrating more on my family and my own children and my parents who were getting older and required more of my attention. I had reconnected with my mother who was alone in Puerto Rico and required a lot of medical attention. I was no longer involved with any particular political organization, but I still belonged to several community boards concentrating more on local community and business issues, and with organizations like the National Puerto Rican Business Council.

After my experiences in my last full-time employment for City Council President Andrew Stein, I decided I no longer wanted to work for any elected official or in City government, and I left my position as the Director of Latino Affairs. My new focus was to build my translation business, Morivivi Language Services, and my new company, Latino Sports Ventures, Inc.

In the late summer of 1995 I had been focusing all my energy on building my company, Latino Sports. During those days, after the mayor, the city council president was the most powerful elected official in the city. In the four years I worked with Stein, I had developed many political contacts beyond my home base of the South Bronx.

My experience working with Stein was quite rewarding. I had always been a Bronx-based activist, but working in City Hall, the center of New York City power, exposed me to a whole different world. I had already tested the waters by jumping from being a hardcore activist who was basically raw in electoral politics to understanding that one had to deal with electoral politics and politicians if one wanted to make positive changes in our communities. My hard core revolutionary politics with its catch-phrases of "pick up the gun," "down with the pigs," or "free Puerto Rico now," had been thawing quite a bit as my children grew older, and I realized I had to provide for a family in a capitalist society that I wanted to change. This hit me loud and clear when my then wife, Liz, and I were looking for a babysitter for our five-year-old son, Julio Antonio. After visiting a few prospects at their homes and finally selecting one, Liz asked me, "why is it that our baby sitter who's on welfare has better furniture than we who have college degrees and professional jobs?"

That was a wake-up call for us to realize that we could remain in the South Bronx, but did not have to continue to live as if we were underground activists, ready to evacuate our apartment at a moment's notice.

I had lived in the South Bronx since I was four years old and I never had any intention of leaving the neighborhood just because I had moved up a few notches on the economic ladder. I went from Cauldwell Avenue in the Mott Haven section of the Bronx, a true symbol of the decay and destruction of the South Bronx that still permeates the minds of many today, to an apartment on the Grand Concourse and 161st Street, the most important avenue in the Bronx. However, leaving an area of the Bronx like Mott Haven did not mean you really left it. You can't leave all your friends, family and contacts behind just because they had not moved up economically or perhaps as fast or as legally as I did. Thus the majority of the people in our circle of friends and family were still living in poverty. They were still living in the projects and in many of the slum buildings we had left. Liz and I never felt that we had to move to a more upscale 914 area code, or leave simply because we had college degrees and good jobs. As activists we were committed to our "hood," to remain in the trenches to help organize, and to raise our children in the real world. We just wanted to move to a somewhat safer area. We knew even then that we were just two paychecks away from poverty ourselves.

Besides these experiences, I also believe that Puerto Ricans have an explosive syndrome that I call the TSA (Taíno, Spaniard, African) blood mixture. That mixture of the peaceful but, analytical Taíno indigenous population of Puerto Rico, the courage of those crazy early Spaniards who broke with all fears to cross the oceans and the incredible strength and willpower of those Africans that survived the most inhuman conditions to arrive as slaves to the new world kicks in once in a while and has made many of us *Boricuas* do some very crazy, but brave things. I believe it's a particular gene that many *Boricuas* (Cubans and Dominicans as well) have, but it only awakens under particular conditions and in some people more than in others. We have seen it in our history from actions like those taken by members of the Puerto Rican Nationalist party fighting for our independence, but which unfortunately were labeled as terrorist attacks and for the most part, kept out of our history books. This syndrome has caused me, on more than one occasion, to stand up to injustices no matter what the odds.

# LATINO SPORTS: MY NEW
## FOCUS FOR SURVIVAL

In 1990, I gave an award to Ruben Sierra, a Texas Rangers baseball player who was overlooked by the Baseball Writers Association of America. The Association's decision to bypass this rising young, black, Puerto Rican star caused the activist in me to act. I came up with the idea to recognize Sierra with an award from his Puerto Rican/Latino community. I named it, Latino MVP. I then developed an entity to present the award and created: Latino Sports Ventures.

After much work, serious negotiations and a little arm-twisting, we had the award ceremony at Yankee Stadium, and the experience made me realize that we should present this award to a Latino athlete every year and not wait for others to recognize Latino role models. Subsequently, I organized three additional awards and was working on the one for 1995 at the time of Fidel's visit to New York. During the days leading up to Fidel's visit I had gone to Boston to meet with some folks to promote Latino Sports. My idea was to expand our reach in Latino communities throughout New England by signing on local Latino newspapers to utilize my Latino Sports news coverage. I had developed a good working relationship with several baseball players, including Puerto Rican, Carlos Baerga who's Cleveland Indians were playing the Atlanta Braves in the World Series. Because of Baerga, I knew that I had a good opportunity to market any event with the Cleveland Indians. I was caught up with that, until I came home from Boston, when I learned about Fidel Castro's visit to New York and Mayor Giuliani's *disrespect* of Cuba's President.

# DAVID GALARZA CALLS TO SAY:
## "THEY INSULTED YOUR BOY"

It was a Thursday night October 19, 1995. I had just returned to my apartment in the Bronx. I received a phone call from my friend, David Galarza. David and I had a working relationship, as we were trying to collaborate on an idea we had to work with *El Diario – La Prensa,* the city's oldest Spanish daily newspaper, to produce a sports section in English. We also had a political relationship as we had both worked for elected officials. David was a writer working in the press office of Manhattan Borough President, Ruth Messinger. Ms. Messinger, a progressive politician whom I respected, was a friend from my days in El Comité. David and I had collaborated occasionally on some of our employers' events. When David called, he said, "Hey, Julio, did you hear how they insulted your boy?" I was totally taken off guard. He asked if I had read the newspapers recently. I told him that since I left my job at Stein's office as Director of Latino Affairs, I read the newspapers from the back pages forward, focusing only on sports.

David explained that the United Nations was celebrating its 50th anniversary and had invited all the world leaders and delegates to attend.[iii] This was an enormously important event that would put New York on the world stage. He explained that Mayor Giuliani had organized a welcome dinner for world leaders, but had *disinvited* Fidel Castro. I told David I was still unclear as to what he thought this action by the mayor had to do with me.

David explained that he believed the mayor was doing this to embarrass Fidel at the request of right-wing Cuban exiles from Miami, Florida, and Union City, New Jersey. There was a rumor circulating that Cuban exile leaders allegedly told the mayor that if he spurned President Castro during his visit to New York, in gratitude they would contribute generously to his future political campaigns.

David suggested that the Latino community should do something to counter the mayor's action against a Latin American head of state. I understood his point. Let's face it, who was the mayor to have a dinner and disinvite any world leader? David added that the mayor also disinvited Palestine Liberation Organization leader, Yasser Arafat.

As a Puerto Rican activist, I shared David's concern. New York had a very large and growing Latino population. To have a Latin American leader come to our city and to have the mayor disinvite this leader to an event he had organized for all the other 180 heads of state and delegates was indeed disrespectful. This disrespect was not just toward Fidel Castro and the people of Cuba, but also against the Latino community of New York City. This was especially true for Puerto Ricans, who comprised the Latino majority and had the most Latino elected officials in the city. While perhaps the mayor was acting on a suggestion from right-wing Cubans who were promoting their anti-communist, anti-Castro rhetoric that has characterized them since the Cuban revolution, this should not have guided his behavior. New York was not Miami, or Union City, New Jersey where the Cuban exile population is larger. They had no strong political or cultural presence in New York.

I was familiar with the perspective of the Cuban exiles. I had encounters with some of their representatives back in the late 1970's when I worked with the Recruitment and Training Program (RTP, Inc.) and represented RTP at the U.S. Youth Council meetings held in Washington, DC. The few Latino representatives in those meetings were one or two delegates from the Mexican-American or Cuban- American communities and me, a Puerto Rican from the South Bronx; three Latino representatives generally on opposite sides of the political spectrum. No matter what conversations we had on issues affecting youth in the country, the Mexican representative and I would always end up taking a liberal position, while the Cuban representatives always taking on a much more conservative position than us.

In the meantime, David continued his efforts to persuade me to do something about the slight to Fidel Castro, instigating me with words like, "If anyone can do this, you can." "You have a lot of contacts with the right people who we can add to a simple news release inviting Fidel Castro. It's not as if he'll really come; it's just an invite." He added something like, "it would show that the Latino community is reacting to the mayor's disrespect." I listened to David's words and I could feel the activist in me slowly resurfacing. I asked David what we needed to do to put out a news release? He said I should find an organization to do the formal invitation, which should include a location for the dinner to show that it was a legitimate proposal.

I belonged to several non-profit organizations, but not one of them was appropriate. Those that received funding from government institutions would not want to risk their funding sources by adding their names to such a press release. Any organization receiving government funds, or affiliated to any city agency would not want to associate with something that was critical of the mayor and as radical as associating with Fidel Castro. Besides, I did not want people to think I was crazy by asking them to put their name on a news release inviting Fidel Castro to dinner. I had to give more thought to whom I could ask to be the sponsoring organization, but pinpointing a location was a lot easier.

I was very close to Jimmy Rodríguez, the owner of the sometimes-controversial Jimmy's Bronx Café. Jimmy's Bronx Café was one of the most popular

Puerto Rican/Latino- owned restaurants in the city. It was the place to be if you were known, or wanted to be known in the community. It was a regular hangout for elected officials, celebrities, and especially baseball players. The latter was partially my doing since I introduced Jimmy to the first professional baseball player to visit his restaurant when I held the first reception of the Latino Most Valuable player award in 1990 at his father's restaurant, *Marisco Del Caribe*, located on Webster Avenue, the predecessor to Jimmy's Bronx Café.[iv]

After that first event, we continued to give the Latino MVP award every year. Through the years, Jimmy and I developed a very close relationship and we started to hold the event at his new place - Jimmy's Bronx Café - a restaurant, sports bar, and catering hall on Fordham Road. I thought that restaurant would be the perfect place to put on our press release as the site for the dinner for President Fidel Castro.

# DAY TWO - THE WORK BEGINS

The following day I went to my office. As usual, my agenda was packed. I had been away for a few days and had a lot of catching up to do. But throughout the day I kept thinking about the previous night's conversation with David Galarza about inviting Fidel Castro to come to the Bronx. Although I was convinced that the Latino community should do something, I was still considering, whether this was the best way to make a statement. My experiences growing up and living in the South Bronx had taught me to always trust my gut. And my gut was telling me that we should not let Mayor Giuliani get away with disinviting President Castro and insulting the Latino community. However, I had to first focus on my work in the office.

When I got home that evening, I continued to think about everything David and I had discussed the previous night. After dinner I again began to concentrate on the idea of writing a news release. The more I thought about David's suggestion of doing what he perceived as a "simple news release" the more my mind filled with all kinds of thoughts. It seemed doable to write a release to show the mayor that he could not speak for the majority of Latinos who lived in the city, especially when no one had spoken up for President Castro. However, I wondered where other Latino leaders, activists, and elected officials stood on this issue and whether anyone would care about a news release criticizing the mayor and inviting President Castro to an event sent out by some folks in the South Bronx. I wondered if any news service would even pick it up. I had worked on countless events and issues that were definitely newsworthy in the past, and we sent out news releases that never got the time of day. It was as if there was an unwritten rule that only negative news gets covered in the Bronx. So I wondered whether anyone would pay attention to a news release about some folks in the South Bronx criticizing the mayor and extending an invitation to President Fidel Castro to visit the borough.

I was no longer involved with electoral politics, but I knew that anything having to do with Cuba and Fidel Castro would be a very sensitive issue. I began to think a lot about the pros and cons of a simple news release that no longer appeared to be that simple to me.

However, the fact that this had to do with Fidel Castro (a man who had been portrayed for so long in such a negative way in the United States, as a communist dictator, who was hated by so many Cuban exiles and misunderstood by so many others) made it a bit more difficult. This was quite different from the countless other issues with which I had been involved throughout the years as an organizer, and sometimes just raising hell in the South Bronx.

Lastly, many of my previous activist events were usually decided by a group of left-leaning individuals like myself. To get others (and in this case more business and professionals with different political views and philosophies) to agree to support this action was going to be one of my greatest challenges.

Here is where I really needed to pull out my graduate MBA notes from New York University on the art of negotiating. However, my years working with Andrew Stein, although frustrating for the most part, had also exposed me to many different sectors of this diversified city, which I felt prepared me for moments like this one.

The more I thought about it, the more convinced I was that we had to do something. I believed that the fallout of not doing anything within the Puerto Rican community would be worse than anything that might occur as a result of writing a news release. As I was still thinking about what to do, I received a phone call that pushed me over the top, and convinced me to make some noise.

## A CALL FROM A FRIEND - IS A CALL
## FOR PUERTO RICANS TO ACT

I received a phone call from my friend, Randy Daniels, inviting me to go to an event with Fidel Castro at the Abyssinian Baptist Church in Harlem. Randy explained that the pastor, Calvin Butts, had told him he could invite a few friends and contacts. Randy and I were good friends and had been business partners in a television venture in Vermont. We became very close when we both worked for City Council President Andrew Stein and Randy was senior press secretary. He was a key member of Stein's' internal staff and had opened the door for me to come in as director of Latino Affairs. Though we no longer worked for Stein, our friendship was solid, like two veterans of a war. During our tenure, he and I consistently collaborated because we were the only two people of color in the senior cabinet of the second most powerful elected official in New York City. We both felt others on his staff had neither a clue about nor any respect for our communities.

When Randy told me about the invitation I was staggered! Here I was thinking about simply preparing a news release criticizing the mayor for disinviting Fidel to his dinner and inviting him to visit the South Bronx, and here was the African-American community inviting me to an actual event that was already confirmed with Fidel's attendance. Fidel was going to Harlem!

I thanked Randy for inviting me to the Harlem event with Fidel and told him I would be honored to attend, but that I preferred to invite Fidel Castro to come to the Bronx for a dinner here with the Puerto Rican community.

I knew that the Cuban government and Fidel had a historic relationship with Harlem. History has documented the importance of Fidel's first visit to Harlem during the U.N. General Assembly in September 1960 as one of the biggest events that ever took place in New York. The Theresa Hotel (now Theresa Towers Office Building) on 125th Street and 7th Avenue was the center of attention when Fidel's entourage moved there after refusing to stay at the midtown Shelburne Hotel on Lexington Avenue and East 37th Street. Castro stormed out of the Shelburne Hotel, after just one night there, when they insisted on a $10,000 bond and Castro complained about the additional surveillance. Castro and his delegation packed up and moved to 125th Street in Harlem to the then Theresa Hotel. Harlem became the center of attention, as Fidel turned that visit into one of the most covered visits of anyone to New York. His decision to move to Harlem blew everyone's mind, including the U.S. Secret Service and the New York Police Department that were responsible for protecting the Cuban leader while he was here for his United Nations visit.

The Harlem community was ecstatic to have a world leader temporarily living among them. The then Theresa Hotel had always been an attraction for famous black leaders from Patrice Lumumba, Malcolm X, Muhammad Ali, A. Phillip Randolph, Lena Horne, and Duke Ellington among others. However, a world figure like Fidel Castro, leader of a successful revolution in the Caribbean and commander of the first liberated territory in the Americas, was something else.

The media and activists who wanted to get a glimpse of Fidel's visit besieged Harlem, the Mecca of Black Power in the Northeast and possibly the nation. The Harlem community loved all the attention it was getting because of it. Harlem was going through its own mini-revolution for community empowerment and Fidel's visit helped bring international attention to a community that was usually ignored. I realized that Harlem already had a history with Fidel Castro. Perhaps writing a news release standing up for President Castro and the progressive Cuban community would help bring that same attention to the South Bronx.

# WHAT FINALLY MADE ME DECIDE: "LET'S DO THIS."

I was astounded by the clear and definitive response of the Harlem leadership and the community at large! Then I looked at the news release we were thinking of doing as our response to Giuliani and that it probably wouldn't go any further than perhaps, *El Diario – La Prensa*, New York's Spanish-language daily.

I had to evaluate what possible repercussions a news release might bring to those that I involved. Personally, I was not afraid of any right wing Cuban exiles since I had no dealings with that community at all (or so I thought, more on this later). My apprehension had to do with the broader political arena. A press release Inviting Fidel Castro to the Bronx was not like anything with which I had previously been involved —protesting a hospital closing, or police brutality, or supporting a community candidate against the insensitive and out-of-touch Bronx Democratic Party organization. This proposed event was bigger than any political event I had ever done before — including my involvement in the takeover of a church in El Barrio on 111th and Lexington Avenue with guns in October 1970 when I was 18 years old, in the second takeover of that church by the Young Lords Party. I was a teenager then, a mere participant, and life and all its repercussions did not hit me as clearly as they did now as an adult with a wife and three children and beginning to start venturing into the business world. In this case I would not be a mere participant, but the catalyst taking on the mayor by extending an invitation to President Fidel Castro.

I was acutely aware that the news release could possibly stir national and international reaction whether Fidel actually came to the Bronx, or not. An invitation to Fidel Castro, probably one of the most misunderstood political figures of the 20th century and the leader of an island nation who had stared down at least nine U.S. presidents over and over again, might get some attention. Fidel was the man who led the campaign to bring into being the first liberated territory in the Americas and who had been on the CIA's hit list for years.[v] The publication of the press release, with or without Fidel's presence in the Bronx, would get the attention needed to at least have the Puerto Rican community appear like we did something.

I knew that Puerto Rico and Cuba had a close relationship as I had heard many times growing up the saying *"Puerto Rico y Cuba, las dos alas del mismo pajaro,"* (Puerto Rico and Cuba the two wings of the same bird). I remember asking David, why me? David knew me well and mentioned the events I had held at Jimmy's with baseball players, my involvement with Carlos Nazario and the National Puerto Rican Business Council (NPRBC). He mentioned a dinner that the council had with members of the Cuban Mission to the United Nations and a reception that I had attended at the Cuban Mission. He also knew of my relationship with several key elected officials. He felt that if anyone could do something, it was I because of the contacts that I had.

Should we let the mayor get away with insulting a Latino, in this case Cuban President Fidel Castro and by extension, the people of Cuba and Latinos in New York City?

I kept thinking of the invitation from Randy Daniels. My mind was going through a lot just thinking about putting this news release together. After talking with Randy about the event planned in Harlem, I was convinced that the Puerto Rican community had to do something. A news release inviting Fidel Castro to the Bronx might just be the right thing to do. It would show that some Puerto Ricans/Latinos did something. If anything, all the attention would probably be on Fidel actually attending an event in Harlem, rather than just an invitation to the South Bronx.

As a Latino, I kept thinking about how it would look to the rest of the country if the Latino community of New York, with its Puerto Rican majority, said or did nothing about Mayor Giuliani's decision to exclude Fidel Castro from the dinner he was offering to other world leaders. I answered my own question and knew it would make us look weak and totally impotent, especially when the African-American community was having Fidel visit Harlem.

It was at that moment that it became more than clear that I had to do it. My past activism, or the streak of the TSA (Taíno, Spaniard, African) syndrome of this Nuyorican kid raised in New York's South Bronx kicked in and convinced me we could not afford to remain quiet. I believed that if we did nothing, progressive Latinos in other parts of the country would ridicule us. They would say that the *Boricuas* (Puerto Ricans who consider themselves progressive) in New York, "*no estaban en na,*" (were not into anything/were weak). That's when I decided that, Hell No! I was going to work on this news release as best as I could.

# CALLING JIMMY TO GET HIS RESTAURANT: JIMMY'S BRONX CAFÉ

It must have been 11:00 p.m. when relentless David Galarza called me again to see where we were with the news release idea. I told him about my conversation with Randy Daniels and my analysis that if we didn't act, New York Latinos, especially *Boricuas* or Puerto Ricans, would appear super weak to all other progressive Latinos throughout the country. So I agreed that we should write the news release.

David told me all we needed was an organization like the National Puerto Rican Business Council (NPRBC), of which I was vice president, to invite President Fidel Castro to the Bronx, and a place to hold an event.

I did not think twice about getting a restaurant, that was easy, in this case, Jimmy's Bronx Café because of my relationship with the owner, Jimmy Rodriguez, and because I had worked with him on other events. I also thought Jimmy was as crazy as us, and would be easy to convince. However, I wasn't as sure about the NPRBC. I knew that was not my call and that it was not going to be easy to convince a bunch of Puerto Rican businessmen interested in building their businesses and making profits to buy into this crazy idea of inviting Fidel Castro, President of the Socialist Republic of Cuba, to the Bronx.

The NPRBC was not apolitical. We had been involved in a number of political issues that affected the organization's members and we had a good working relationship with many elected officials in the Bronx. On occasion, we also had been invited to cultural receptions at the Cuban mission to the U.N. However, that was totally different from being the group to criticize the mayor and invite President Fidel Castro to the Bronx. The fact that most of the leadership was Republican was not exactly encouraging. I thought that getting approval would be difficult, if not impossible, and that the idea was probably not going to fly with the organization at all. The only hope was that I had a very good and close working relationship with our President, Carlos Nazario who was not your typical conservative Republican. In fact, Carlos did some radical things himself by having our organization take on mighty Anheuser Busch on a pricing plan that was going to put many beer wholesalers out of business. After successfully helping Anheuser Busch introduce their brand to the community, Anheuser Busch decided to set up a predatory pricing plan to sell directly to the grocery stores at a lower price than to the wholesalers. This practice was responsible for putting many Latino-owned wholesalers out of business.

I was reluctant to pursue the NPRBC route; however, David insisted it would make the news release more credible and it would be taken seriously, if it came from a recognized business organization rather than a general invite from a no-name group, or myself and my small start up, Latino Sports. I told him I would think about it, but asked him to first let me concentrate on getting Jimmy's Bronx Café to be the event venue and sign on to the news release.

I knew that Jimmy was less concerned about political repercussions than the publicity he would get for the restaurant. If anything, naming his restaurant as the venue, would get Jimmy's Bronx Café mentioned in the Spanish dailies, giving him free publicity, something he loved more than his delicious empanadas.

I called Jimmy close to midnight, which was by habit the best time to reach him. He answered the phone and greeted me with his usual, "what's up?"

I brought him up to speed about how the mayor had disinvited Fidel and that I thought that we Puerto Ricans had a great opportunity to put our neglected borough on the map. I spoke to Jimmy from a marketing angle. I told him what he already knew, that the Bronx needed more positive attention. I told him that the more attention we got for the Bronx, the more attention he would get for his restaurant, which would mean more customers for him and a better image of our 'hood,' I told him. "Jimmy, this is a win-win situation."

Jimmy paused a bit and told me he did not know if this was a good idea for the restaurant. I reminded him that this was a just a news release mentioning his business as the possible venue and was not committing him, or the restaurant to anything, except free publicity. Jimmy was also a member of the National Puerto Rican Business Council, so I told him that I was also going to reach out to Carlos Nazario, our president, and ask for the organization's support.

Jimmy then said something to the effect of: "you know they have accused the restaurant of so many negative things, a place for 'unsavory characters,' so what the hell, they can't say anything worse. Go ahead put me down."[vi] So I thought, "Hooray, I did it, I got it! We have a location, now for the big one, the National Puerto Rican Business Council."

# GETTING THE SUPPORT OF THE NATIONAL PUERTO RICAN BUSINESS COUNCIL

Getting the support of the National Puerto Rican Business Council was going to be more difficult. First I had to convince our President, Carlos Nazario. Although we were at opposite ends of the political spectrum — Carlos was a Republican and I was a registered Democrat — we had a very good working relationship and shared many similar traits. We were both Taurus, and in fact we share a birthday, April 29. But in a strange way, the political differences and personal similarities balanced themselves out quite well.

I came from a revolutionary leftist background living all my life in the South Bronx. Carlos came from a more conservative background, living in up-state New York, with a business in the South Bronx. I was an *Independentista* wanting independence for Puerto Rico and he was an *Estadista* wanting statehood for Puerto Rico. But despite holding conflicting political ideals, we had an incredible close relationship and had similar thoughts on all the issues affecting our daily lives and our South Bronx community. Carlos and I worked very closely together, so much so that when we started the NPRBC, Carlos recommended me as vice president. He knew my revolutionary background and did not flinch at the idea of having me serve as vice president. In fact, it was because of Carlos Nazario, that I was able to expand my sense of what business relationships could be, and I began opening up to the idea of talking to others who might have totally different political opinions from mine. The NPRBC helped me expand my progressive community activist ideology to include more business relationships. I learned to look beyond party lines, and be open to people and not just a party, or political platform. Carlos was the person partly responsible for expanding my tolerance of non-leftist ideologies. Thanks to the NPRBC, I stopped thinking along electoral party lines. I was not a Democratic Party loyalist, but in the Bronx if you were not a Democrat you could not vote in the Democratic primaries where the real election takes place. When I first registered to vote at the age of 28, I registered as an Independent. I only switched to Democrat when I wanted to help José Serrano run for borough president in 1985. (Also for another story).

Though I might have been able to convince Carlos, I knew that he would probably not want to make the decision to put the organization's name on a news release inviting President Fidel Castro on his own. I knew that as president he was not going to make a major decision without the approval of the executive board, which would require a meeting of at least a quorum. The executive team included Ralph Declet, who ran a small Bronx consulting firm; Tony Rodríguez, owner of two McDonald's restaurants in the South Bronx; Carlos Nazario, who owned, Metro Beer and Soda Distributors on River Avenue and 149th St; and myself, owner of Morivivi Language Services, a small interpreting firm and a start-up, Latino Sports, both located on 149th Street. I had a good relationship with all of them; they always showed patience and took the time to deal with my sometimes-strong radical points of view and had supported several of my events and sponsored some of my projects. However, this was not going to be something simple like sponsoring my radio program, or a luncheon with a baseball player for South Bronx kids. This was something that included the name Fidel Castro and that alone would raise many eyebrows and concerns. Some members of the council had attended smaller events held by the Cuban Mission to the United Nations. I had introduced to them through my friend and contact Franklin Flores, who had close contacts with the Cuban Mission. We had been invited to receptions where we had met Cuban members of the Mission, and we had invited some of them to the South Bronx where we had given visiting delegates a tour. As progressive as those actions might have been, I saw them as baby steps compared to what I was about to ask them to do.

I had called Carlos the day after speaking to David to follow up on other council matters. We had touched the issue of Mayor Giuliani's decision to disinvite President Castro to the dinner for visiting dignitaries. That was big news in the Latino community and it ran a lot on Spanish radio and television stations. But that was just chitchat about the political happenings of the city. I had mentioned something about Latinos doing something, but nothing specific. Now I was ready to speak to him because I had something more concrete with the information that President Castro was going to Harlem and that the owner of Jimmy's Bronx Café, one of our members, was on board to put his name on the news release. With myself, that would be two of us from the council.

This second call now was specifically on the issue of the news release. I told him of the plan and pointed out that the NPRBC had the opportunity to put our organization's name out there and jump to the forefront of the Latino business community. I said this was in line with what the black community was doing in Harlem, except that we were not a church inviting Fidel, but a business organization. The first thing he said to me, was, "are you crazy," but being a very intelligent business leader, Carlos immediately picked up on the political angle of this action.

The NPRBC was a new and fast growing organization of Puerto Rican business owners. We were competing with many other business organizations and Chambers of Commerce that had more seniority and access than our new organization. The Cuban exile community in Miami and Union City had business councils; the new and growing Dominican community had two business councils in New York and the Mexican-Americans had the greatest number of business councils in various southwestern states and in California. The Puerto Rican community here in New York was the only one that did not have a business council, which was the main reason that Carlos got us all to go along with him and start the NPRBC.

Carlos was an astute businessman and politically savvy. He saw that just by having our organization's name on a news release inviting someone like Fidel to come to the Bronx could spotlight the NPRBC and give it the potential to become one of the premier Latino business organizations in the city and possibly in the Northeast.

We both concluded that Castro would never come to the Bronx. Why would he come to the Bronx to meet with a group called the National Puerto Rican Business Council? Besides, we believed that his schedule was already planned and would not permit for any last minute additions.

However, Carlos said the words I was looking for: "Hey why not. Let's give it a shot, let's give it a try!" GREAT! The President of the NPRBC is with me on this idea! But now we had to convince the board. Carlos wanted to have a special executive session to ask the board for approval.

# PRESIDENT OF THE NPRBC CALLS A SPECIAL
# MEETING OF THE EXECUTIVE BOARD

Carlos did not waste any time and by early afternoon he had called an executive board meeting. Since several members were out of town, or far from the Bronx where we usually met, we had a conference call meeting. Carlos started the conference call explaining that this was just about one item and he presented the idea that he and I had already agreed upon. That started a little debate among the members. I remember someone saying that we were a business group that supported capitalism, so why were we interested in adding our name to an invitation for a communist? Carlos explained the political actions behind our move. We also reiterated the obvious; that Fidel would not be coming. This was just a news release. I mean Carlos was right. Who were we? We were a South Bronx-based Puerto Rican business group getting off the ground. We had no major contacts or relationships with the Cuban government. Our few encounters with the Cuban Mission to the United Nations were minor, and more of a political courtesy.

I took the opportunity to explain the benefits of being the official organization to invite Fidel Castro to the Bronx from a business perspective. I explained from what I had read in the papers that Castro was going to attend several meetings during his five days in New York. I explained that he was a friend of Ted Turner and that he was probably going to have meetings with Anglo businessmen. I reminded them of an article that had appeared in Newsweek months earlier about Chrysler Chairman, Lee Iacocca visiting with Castro in Havana. This was one of those times that I realized how important it was to be well read and informed. I explained that if we put the National Puerto Rican Business Council's name on the news release as the inviting organization, it could help us open the doors for possible business opportunities in Cuba in the not-too-distant future. I also remember mentioning the respect that we would get from other Latino businesses that probably would agree with our position, but might be afraid to say anything, since no other Latino entity had come out with any statement yet, other than radicals or activists. I heard some react immediately to my comment. One member said, "Yeah how will this help us?"

I remember Tony Rodríguez asking, "Will they allow me to open a McDonald's in Havana?" I responded, "No not now Tony, but think about this. If we are on record for inviting Fidel to the Bronx, our organization will be remembered as a friend of the Cuban revolution. At present there is a U.S. Blockade against the Cuban government and there can be no business between us".

Then I asked, "What will happen when this Blockade that has not worked in all these years finally comes down?" I had their attention and continued, "The Cubans will want to do business with businesses and people that have been friendly to their government. They are not going to do business with the Cuban exile community in Miami that has done everything possible to destroy them." I added, that my understanding was that the Cuban government was very principled and loyal to those they considered friends. I added that they were probably already looking for organizations in the United States that they could do business with if and when the blockade was lifted. I stressed, "If we add our name to this press release as being the organization that invites Fidel while he was disinvited by the mayor we would be on a list of principled organizations that the Cuban government would want to consider doing business with once the U.S. Blockade comes down." Carlos reiterated that Fidel also had been invited to events by several Anglo business organizations and it seemed that with the black community inviting him to Harlem, we (the Latino community) were the only ones not inviting him.

It seemed we had made a good argument. Carlos called for a vote and to my surprise it was unanimous, a 4-0 vote to be the official organization to invite Fidel Castro to the Bronx. The news release was a go. They also allocated $500 for a banner and any other expenses that might have to be incurred in case we needed to have a news conference. I was so happy! I got four Republicans to endorse and support our crazy, but courageous invitation to President Fidel Castro, a Cuban leader invited by the United Nations, but insulted by our mayor. We could now go forward with the news release.

# DAVID GALARZA UPS THE ANTE

So here I was, as happy as an activist can be. I got a location and I got an official organization to actually sign on as the host of a dinner for Fidel Castro. So I thought, now let's do this! I called David and gave him the good news. Fidel was scheduled to arrive on Saturday October 23, and we had accomplished our goal in record time. We had what we needed to write and send out the news release before Fidel's arrival.

David was as elated as I was, but he threw one more hurdle in the way. He said that before writing the news release, I should add one more person to the host committee, because not only would it be a good thing to do, but also it might guarantee that the news release would get published. I asked, who? He answered, Congressman José Serrano. I told David that was not going to happen. I said I had not heard of any elected official in the Bronx, or in the city, criticizing the mayor's action. While he might have a good idea, trying to get Congressman Serrano to support this news release was probably not going to work. Besides, I told him, just trying to get to Congressman Serrano was going to be difficult. Though I had a good relationship with Serrano, it sometimes took me a while to get him to return a call.

I had known Congressman Serrano since 1975, when I was a teenager, before he was an Assemblyman. I knew him to be super-cautious on everything he did. In my opinion, supporting something like this for Fidel Castro was definitely something that Congressman Serrano might not be too willing to do. I had a special relationship with him that went back decades since my years as an undergraduate student and when I lived on Cauldwell Avenue (again, story for another day). I campaigned and voted for Serrano, the first time I had ever done this for an elected official. We had kept a close relationship throughout the years. In those early years I had always told him that if he ever decided to run independently of the Bronx Democratic County organization of then County Chair Stanley Friedman, I would help him. In 1985 he called and invited me to Albany, so he could talk to me about something. I hated Albany, since I only went there for demonstrations and in the winter it was too damned cold. However, this was the first time anyone had personally invited me there, and I was curious to know why.

Once I got there, we met and Serrano reminded me of my promise to support him if he ever ran against the county political machine. He told me he was tired of being promised the Bronx Borough Presidency and that they had reneged twice on that promise. Therefore, he was going to run against the Bronx County Democratic organization's candidate, Stanley Simon for borough president. I did not hesitate and immediately told him that I would help his campaign. I had never campaigned for any politician before and knew nothing about elections, but I was well connected in the neighborhood where I had been living since 1956, something that Serrano knew about me, since 1973, when we first met. Serrano asked me what I wanted if he won. I did not understand his question, as I had never been exposed to the backroom deals of electoral politics. He made it clear, explained and asked me again, "What would you want?" I remembered his puzzled look when I answered that all I wanted was all the signs on the bridges and highways that lead to the Bronx that read, "Welcome to the Bronx," and give the Borough President's name, to read, "Welcome to the Bronx/*Bienvenido al Condado Del Bronx*." He asked, "That's it?" I said yes. He wrote some notes down on a piece of paper and then he said out loud, "that was easy." We then went to the state legislative chambers where we took a picture of the two of us sitting in the empty chamber. He later sent a copy to me with the following inscription: "I remember a time when you were not allowed near the state capitol" and signed it, "José Serrano."

Serrano and I were like hand in glove in his campaign for borough president. We hit the streets like a well-coordinated tag team. Yes, we lost, but our campaign was historic; we were outspent by close to $1 million for Stanley Simon to $60,000 for Serrano. Serrano was not expected to get more than perhaps 15 percent of the vote since he did not have even one Bronx elected official supporting him. Everyone was shocked when the South Bronx vote came out in droves like never before, practically equal to the largest borough voter block, Co-Op City. This had never occurred before. Serrano lost that election, but we all knew it was not because of votes, but because of something that has allegedly happened time and time again in the Bronx. He lost that election in the polling stations.

I later worked as director of his constituent office when he was in the state assembly. My family regarded Serrano as family. He had broken bread in my home when I was a college student and years later when we were practically neighbors in my apartment at 888 Grand Concourse. Having worked for Serrano and knowing him personally, I was convinced that Serrano would probably not want to be part of this crazy idea. However, David urged me to try anyway. I remember David saying that Serrano had been vocal on some pro-Cuban issues and I knew he had been vocal against the blockade and on the impending Helms-Burton Act (a federal law that strengthened the embargo against Cuba). David believed that if he supported those issues, he might support this news release. I agreed to try and contact Serrano. However, I knew Serrano was extremely busy and sometimes my calls to Serrano's office would get lost in a void and if and when he did return my call it was no longer relevant. I felt that at least I would try. We needed to get the news release out ASAP and we were not going to wait long to add Serrano's name to it. If we wanted this press release to be effective it had to go out before Fidel arrived in New York City on Saturday.

I called Serrano's office immediately after getting off the phone with David. I told his staff person that I had something very important to discuss with the Congressman, and mentioned that my call had something to do with the mayor's insult to President Fidel Castro before his pending visit and that we were planning to do something about it. I was pleasantly surprised when Serrano called me back just a few hours later. I thanked him for his timely response and proceeded to explain the urgency. I remember going over the details and asking, "Would you want to add your name to a news release that we want to send out inviting Fidel Castro to the Bronx for a dinner in response to the mayor disinviting him to the dinner that he's having for all heads of state?" Serrano said, "Are you serious?" (I believe that "serious" was his courteous word for not also saying, "crazy"). I laughed as that seemed to be a rehearsed line and the initial reaction every time I first mentioned it to anyone. I said I was serious and that I had already secured a restaurant, Jimmy's Bronx Café. Serrano liked Jimmy Rodríguez a lot and frequented his restaurant routinely. I also mentioned that I had spoken to Carlos Nazario and that the National Puerto Rican Business Council would be the official organization making the invitation.

Serrano was aware that I was starting a new business and I believe he was genuinely concerned that this might hurt both my translation business and the new start-up, Latino Sports. I told him that I had no business dealings with the Cuban exile community and that there were no large concentrations of Cuban exiles living in the Bronx that we needed to fear. Besides, I reminded him that this was just a news release. I remember saying, "What are they going to do, criticize our news release?" Serrano basically told me, "I think you're taking a risk, but if you want to do this, I give you permission to add my name to the news release." I was more than surprised! I really did not expect Serrano to sign on because I believed as a Congressman and public figure he would probably get more heat from the Cuban exile community than any of us would.

The fact was that there was no mention of any organization, elected official, activist, or community leader in the city or state saying anything about the mayor disinviting a Latino world leader to his dinner. By signing on to our news release, Serrano was the only elected official to stand up to the mayor on this issue, while bringing additional heat from a vocal and politically connected Cuban exile community that had a lot more influence in Washington than in New York and the South Bronx.

Now I had gotten everything that David had suggested that we needed to give the news release credibility. I got the location, Jimmy's Bronx Café. I got the National Puerto Rican Business Council to be the official organization to host the event and now Congressman José Serrano had agreed to add his name to the invite. Now I thought we could write the news release and send it out and I could return to my daily work. I needed to get my attention back to my businesses as I had been spending a lot more time on this simple news release than I had expected. It turned out not to be that simple after all.

I called David Galarza with the good news. "I got Serrano," I told him. He laughed and told me, "You see, I told you. Now we have all we need to get some serious attention for this news release." David wrote the release and, he faxed me a copy. I liked it and sent it to Carlos Nazario and Congressman Serrano for one last look before we would send it out to the media.

Serrano did not get back to us with his approval until the next day. We had sent the original to him after 5 p.m. Thursday, which is when David was able to work on our project since he could not do this while on the clock at the Manhattan Borough President's office.

Upon getting the final approval with no changes from Serrano or Carlos, we sent the release out to all the media on Friday morning, one day before President Fidel Castro was to arrive in New York. All the faxes were sent from my office and boy was I relieved when it was done and I could say, "Mission accomplished." I then told my daughter, Kimberly, who was working with me at the time, that we could now return to business as usual. She was happy to hear that because I had been basically MIA (Missing In Action) for the last few days. Ever since David's first call, my attention had been focused outside the office on the news release.

By mid-afternoon Kimberly was after me about other business matters that I had not addressed, and she gave me a slew of messages and said I had to return many phone calls.

However, to my surprise we also got a few calls asking about the invite. I was surprised because the news release had been sent out only a few hours earlier. I could not understand how people already knew about it. I called a few friends to ask if they had heard anything on any news station that I might have missed. But word began to spread as soon as we sent out the release. We also verbally told others about it, like Franklin Flores, who had a close relationship with Casa De Las Americas, a civic organization of pro-Cuba supporters, and a few other family and friends, like Maxi Rivera, a South Bronx community activist.

*El Diario* reporter, Gerson Borrero was the first to call my office. He had called before we sent out the release. He asked me about the invite. At that time I declined to comment because we had not yet issued the release. I thought that the less time people knew about our action, the less time people opposed to what we were doing had to react.

We found Gerson's call strange, since he knew about the news release before we had sent it out. That was Gerson, always getting the scoop on the political issues in the Latino community. In this case we believed we knew his source. We believed that Serrano probably called Gerson right after he hung up with me, to give him the exclusive.

We did not have a problem with that, but discipline has always been one of my strongest virtues and I wanted to follow the script we had agreed upon.

Though my name was on the news release, I did not want to be the spokesperson. I believed that Carlos, as president of the sponsoring organization, and Congressman Serrano should be the ones to address the media. I believed my job was to screen and refer any valid requests for comments to either of them.

I also did not want to give out any information until we were ready. This was also a security issue for me. My work in leftist organizations was colored by an atmosphere of super-secrecy. We were taught to give out information only when we absolutely had to do so, and only when we were ready. I wanted to control when and how the information got out. This was no longer possible. The news was out. "Castro Invited to the Bronx" was the word out on the street. As many of us had learned, *"Radio Bemba"* (Gossip Radio) has always had a better reach in our community than the regular news outlets.

# SE FORMÓ EL TIN TIN GO (ALL HELL BREAKS LOOSE)

I don't believe that we had more than a few hours of peace before the storm hit. The release went out Friday early morning and by Friday late morning we began to receive phone calls.

By the next day, it got worse. We got a slew of phone calls related to the release and a few from friends congratulating us for standing up to Mayor Giuliani. I never imagined such a reaction. But Fidel was scheduled to arrive that day, and perhaps that was another reason for the calls. Many of the reporters wanted to know if we had received a response from Fidel, or the Cubans regarding our invitation. Those were easy questions to field, and I did not have to refer them to Carlos, or Serrano.  I just told them, NO.

I left the office after lunch for a meeting. When I returned late afternoon, Kimberly had a look of frustration on her face. She usually looked like that whenever we had a major problem with a bill collector, or an interpreter for our interpreting business that didn't show for an assignment. But this was not one of those problems. Kimberly was frustrated because she said the phones hadn't stopped ringing all morning. Most of the calls, 99 percent, were related to the press release inviting Fidel Castro to the Bronx. Apparently, many more people were interested in the event than we had anticipated. Was Mr. Castro confirmed? What was the NPRBC? What date was the event? What were we going to serve? How much were the tickets to the dinner? Where can they buy a ticket? All of this for something that we truly believed was not happening. We thought all we had done was to put out a news release to make a statement with an invitation to an event we never expected to materialize.

I thought I had prepared my office and Kimberly well for a slight increase in calls. I mean we had sent many other press releases for some of our own events with Latino Sports dealing with major league baseball players who were very popular. As a result, Kimberly had become quite good at handling the media. However, none of us imagined that this news release would create such turmoil in my office.

I advised Kimberly to take messages for all calls related to the Fidel news release so we could go over them at the end of the day, so our regular work would not be interrupted. I told her that depending on the message we could either send them to Carlos Nazario at the NPRBC, or to Congressman Serrano's office. Unfortunately, if I thought that the calls were the only major inconvenience to come out of that news release, I had another thing coming.

# THE LADY IN RED

By late afternoon, the avalanche of phone calls coming into the office had subsided a little. It appeared that things might be returning to normal. There were fewer calls and those that came in were easily manageable. Therefore, I resumed my regular schedule to drum up business for my two small companies. There were hundreds of attorneys along 149th Street, Third Avenue, the Grand Concourse and around the area of 161st Street where I had personally dropped off literature to introduce my interpreting and translation business. After leaving the city council president's office, I decided I no longer wanted to work for anyone again, especially a politician. I began paying a lot of attention to my small interpreting business that I had been running on a part-time basis and also to building up my new company, Latino Sports, to develop it into something more than an organization that honored Latino athletes with annual awards. This was something I had been doing since 1990, when I organized the first award for Ruben Sierra at Yankee Stadium. Developing the interpreting business from the ground up required a lot of my time. I was out in the field most mornings and into the early afternoon, walking and visiting the offices of local attorneys. I had some leads and was looking forward to following up my leads, which I did in the late afternoons when it was easier to talk to attorneys back from court, or to their secretaries, because they were not as busy as in the mornings. However, this was not going to happen that afternoon. I had just sat down at my desk, when Kimberly entered my cubicle and yelled out, "Pa, I forgot to tell you that you need to call Serrano right away, he called several times while you were out and did not want to leave a message."

So again, I put my regular work aside and called Serrano. I did not get a word in when Serrano said in a very serious tone, "I have to tell you something and please listen. When I was about 14 years old" - (I think that was the age he said -) "and living in the Millbrook projects I would always see this very attractive women with a red dress returning home on Saturday in the very early morning hours. She was very attractive and had an incredible body." I couldn't believe this. I had so much work to do, and I had put my work aside to call Serrano for what I believed to be an urgent call, and now he was telling me a childhood story. I did not want to be disrespectful, but I interrupted Serrano and asked him to get to the point, as I had to catch up with a lot of work. He raised his voice and said, "Just listen to me." He continued, "I had a crush on this woman and would dream about one day asking her out on a date." Again I interrupted and said, "José." Again he told me in a hurried anxious tone to be quiet and listen. He continued, "I finally got the courage to ask her out," he said. So now I'm really into his story and asked him, "So, what happened?" Serrano yelled out, "**she said yes.**" I asked him, "And what did you do?" Serrano said, "I ran away!" I was already a bit confused with his story, and now I was totally baffled and somewhat frustrated. But I wanted to know now why he had called me so many times to tell me his childhood story about this attractive lady in the red dress. So I said, "Jose, I don't understand. What does this have to do with me?" I don't believe that I finished my sentence when he blurted out: **"FIDEL SAID YES!"**

"*Que Que*, what?" I yelled out. "Holy shit, are you serious?" "Fidel said yes," he repeated. But how, why? Now my head was really spinning. I was really confused because all I know is that we wrote a news release and we sent it out to the local press. What, why and how does a release meant for the media get to the level where the Cuban President accepts our invitation?

Now, I understood Serrano's story of the lady in red. Serrano never expected her to actually agree to go out with him. Therefore, when the lady answered yes, he ran away. The difference this time was that neither he, nor the National Puerto Rican Business Council, nor I could run away from this. We had to move forward with something that was totally unexpected and for which we were totally unprepared.

# IS THIS REAL? FIDEL CASTRO IS COMING TO THE SOUTH BRONX

The only thing that was going through my head was "Fidel is coming." I also had a slight sense of numbness that one sometimes gets when something happens that is so unexpected, you're still not sure it really happened; when your brain is trying to connect with the rest of your senses asking, "Is this real, or not?" During those few seconds when my mind was going through that, all I remember hearing was a barrage of questions and statements from Serrano. "Do you know what this can do to me, what that's going to cause?" He went on, "This is going to bring demonstrations, pickets, people and press asking all sorts of embarrassing questions." By now my numbness was wearing off as my friend Congressman José Serrano shared his anxieties. Though he had a basis for concern, and as controversial as Fidel Castro might be, I knew the streets of the South Bronx. I could not imagine busloads of Cuban exiles coming to our hood to protest Fidel's visit. The Bronx, with its heavy Puerto Rican and progressive influence, was not exactly a safe haven for conservative right-wing Cubans whose views often clashed with ours.

I settled Serrano when I said, "José, relax we are not going to have any Cuban exile demonstrations here in the South Bronx, I can assure you of that." However, Serrano was on a roll. He went on and asked me, "Yeah, well how are we going to prevent the press, or people standing up and asking Fidel embarrassing questions like," "When are you going to have free elections in Cuba?"

That was a legitimate question. I reminded Serrano that this was a private, not a public dinner, or event. I reminded him of the news release. Nowhere on it, did it say that this was a public event, or how many people were going to be present. This seemed to relax Serrano a bit and he asked me about our guest list and who was going to be there. I reminded him that this was a dinner sponsored by the National Puerto Rican Business Council. Therefore, this dinner could just be between some of our members and some members of his staff, without anyone else being invited. I reminded Serrano that between the many organizations that we had been working with in the South Bronx we could easily fill a room with our people, who were going to be respectful. This really calmed Congressman Serrano and for the first time since our conversation began, we went from panic mode to a calmer planning mode. I then took the opportunity to ask him, how in the world this happened and when is this dinner supposed to take place? I also wanted to know how was it that Fidel accepted an invitation issued through our news release to the local media? Serrano then explained what happened.

## HOW FIDEL CASTRO GOT A COPY
## OF OUR PRESS RELEASE?

We had accepted the fact that Fidel had said yes to our invitation and had committed to come to the Bronx. Now I was concerned about 'what when and how'. Again, I asked Congressman Serrano how this happened?

He told me that he had sent a copy of the release to the Cuban Interest Section, the de facto diplomatic mission in Washington, DC.[vii] Apparently Serrano had several dealings with the Cuban Interest Section and its head, Minister, Fernando Remírez. Thus, as a gesture of courtesy, Serrano had faxed over the copy of our news release to the Cuban Interest Section in Washington, DC.

While in Cuba doing research for this book, I was able to interview Remírez who is now retired. This is his account of the events that led to President Fidel Castro's visit to the Bronx.

Mr. Remírez explained that he was in New York waiting to brief President Castro upon his arrival on that Saturday — October 21, 1995. He said he received a copy of the release from the Washington office and that he had also read it in the paper and heard about it from other sources at the Cuban Mission in New York.[viii] He also recalled that he had received a call from Congressman Serrano regarding the invitation. Serrano was a standing member of the U.S. Congress, who was considered a friend of the Cuban people and that carried a lot of respect. Remírez said he personally gave a copy of the news release to Fidel while briefing him when he arrived from the airport that afternoon.

He told me that Fidel read it and without hesitation said that he would attend. Apparently the decision to attend was made solely by Fidel himself. He did not consult with anyone; he just read the press release and said he was going. According to Remírez, Fidel was in the minority, as other members of the Cuban delegation as well as the Secret Service from both countries were uncomfortable with Fidel attending. However, Fidel's decision won out, and that's how President Fidel Castro wound up coming to the South Bronx dinner. According to Remírez that was "quite unusual." He explained that all of President Castro's meetings in New York were planned and approved far in advance. The fact that President Castro spontaneously decided to attend an event that was not on his previously arranged agenda, for which he had not been briefed by anyone on his staff, was quite unusual. This was symbolic of the relationship that Cuba and Puerto Rico have always had. I believe that upon reading the news release it must have had a special meaning to President Castro, when he learned was that it was a Puerto Rican event sponsored by the National Puerto Rican Business Council (NPRBC), supported by Congressman José Serrano, a Puerto Rican, and that the dinner would be held in the heart of the largest Puerto Rican community in the United States, the South Bronx. President Castro has always demonstrated Cuba's internationalism and solidarity. I also believe that President Castro saw in our invitation the warmth of a community that was as close to his home, Cuba, as he would experience in his five-day visit to New York. In addition, the fact the invitation was mainly a response to the mayor's insensitivity must have also played into the analytical and intuitive mind of President Castro.[ix]

Serrano had also explained that when Fidel was given a copy of the press release he stated: *"Dile a mis hermanos puertorriqueños que estaré allí con ellos, que para mi esto es cómo recibir un premio Nobel"* (Tell my Puerto Rican brothers that I will be there with them and that for me this is like receiving a Nobel prize).

After hearing Serrano's explanation as to how he believed the press release got into Fidel Castro's hands, I was stunned and a bit confused. I wanted to ask him why would he share our news release in Washington, DC, or why would he send it out beyond the comfort zone of our New York City area? Our release was supposed to be a reaction to Mayor Rudolph Giuliani's *snub* of President Castro from the dinner planned for all heads of state, *not* an actual dinner invitation for President Fidel Castro. At no point had we actually thought of having a dinner. However, I also knew that as a legislator, Serrano did what he believed was the right thing for him to do. I realized that as a congressman who had communications with the Cuban Interest Section, Serrano had an obligation to share that press release with them.

The invitation to invite President Fidel Castro to visit the Bronx went way beyond the Bronx, and Serrano as the Congressman was one of the conduits. However, now because he had allowed us to add his name to a simple news release in response to Giuliani's' insult to Fidel, it had now become a formal invitation that had left the confines of the South Bronx and gotten into the hands of one of the most controversial political figures in the world, President Fidel Castro.

I also remember the second shock, when Serrano told me the dinner had to take place on Monday, October 23. That meant that we had approximately 72 hours to organize the event. The timing was short, but in my mind I was thinking that between the NPRBC and Serrano's staff we could easily plan a small dinner without any major problems. I first would have to call the other parties, Carlos Nazario and Jimmy Rodríguez, and tell them the good news — or the bad news — depending on how they would interpret it.

I really did not think much of the dinner logistics, the timeframe, or of the major impact of Fidel Castro coming to the South Bronx. My mind was still thinking of Fidel's comment, *"Tell my Puerto Rican brothers that I will be there with them and that for me this is like receiving a Nobel Prize."* Fidel's comment was so unexpected and so uncharacteristic to what we have all been told about him that it touched me deeply. Though I had been exposed to many of Fidel's speeches and much of his writings through my past affiliation with revolutionary organizations like the Young Lords and El Comité - MINP, I had never heard anything, or read something from Fidel as poetic and warm as those words that were directed exclusively to us. The fact that he compared receiving our simple press release, turned invitation to receiving a Nobel Prize was the ultimate. The feeling was overwhelming. I could not help thinking that a press release written to respond to a local issue of our mayor disinviting a Latin American leader had actually become a formal invitation, now in Fidel Castro's hands, and that now it could become a national, or perhaps even an international issue. I smiled as I thought that if anything, the South Bronx was going to be a talking point in the news for the next couple of days, and not just as another negative news story. Perhaps like Fidel's first visit to Harlem in 1960, our *Condado De La Salsa* was going to go Prime Time news.

However, that telephone conversation with Congressman Serrano and the subsequent days leading up to that conversation, were nothing compared with what awaited me over those next 70 - something hours.

***

# BREAKING THE NEWS, ONE
# PERSON AT A TIME

As soon as I got over the initial trauma that Fidel was actually coming to the Bronx, I immediately shifted gears to plan what we never thought we would have to do, organize a dinner for Fidel Castro. I called Kimberly into my office and told her the good/bad news. To her credit and my surprise she did not react in any way other than basically to shrug her shoulders and think, "OK, another event that was not planned and we have less than three days to organize and put it together." Kimberly is my first-born and had been introduced to all my political wheeling's and dealings right from the start. I took her and her younger sister, Taína, to just about every event that I attended, from the time they began to walk — demonstrations, meetings and even college at the ages of four and five, when I was in my senior year at Lehman College and we could not afford a babysitter. My Lehman college SEEK counselor, Socorro Texidor, would not let me use them as an excuse to miss class, so she had me bring them to her office on campus, and she would watch them while I attended classes.

By the time I started my businesses, both of them were in their early teens, but with more knowledge about business responsibilities than most kids their age. Both of them and their younger brother, Julio Antonio, had early introductions to community politics and business development. At one time or the another, they had been with me to hand out flyers in the streets, collect petitions for some cause, answer phones, file papers, stuff envelopes, or just do general office work. Kimberly was the first to begin working full time with me, juggling a little of my language service business and a lot more on the new start-up, Latino Sports. She had worked on many of our events, many of which had been eleventh hour, demanding a quick turn around, and almost all photo finish. I guess all of that work helped forge the young lady who was now looking at me with no emotion, saying, "What else is new." Kimberly was immune to my anxiety over shifting gears from all our other work to organizing this dinner for Fidel Castro. Kimberly was looking at this as just another event, and did not see the potential turmoil that this could cause, and I was glad for that. I had always guarded my children from much of my involvement with internal, more serious politics. My children had a general good understanding of leftist politics, but in this case Kimberly was unaware of the ramifications that a Fidel Castro visit might have and I wanted to keep it that way. Kimberly was developing into a good manager and events planner with solid, disciplined skills. I saw no need to alarm her by sharing the political details of this dinner. I sat down with her and divided the tasks of looking over our contact list of close friends and family, while preparing a list of people we trusted who we might want to invite and put on a possible stand-by list, just in case we had to fill the dinner with our personal contacts. To her this was just another last-minute event we had to organize, and like the good trooper she was, she complied.

# GUESS WHO'S COMING TO DINNER?

The first question that Serrano had raised after we both got over the initial shock of "FIDEL SAID YES!" was to start thinking about who to invite to the dinner. We only had about 72 hours to put this event together and it had to be flawless, nothing could go wrong (This was at a time when we had no "smart phones", internet, emails, etc.). Serrano's point was that he did not want to be embarrassed and I took that to another level. I believed none of us could be embarrassed and nothing should go wrong. Period.

That's when I decided to call on those people I considered the "inner core." Those were the individuals that I had worked with, or convinced to sign on to the news release. I got on the phone and called David Galarza. He had put this crazy idea in my head and according to him this was just going to be a "press release" to show up the mayor. I wanted him to know that this was now much more. This was now an invitation that had been taken seriously and what we thought would never happen, was happening. Fidel Castro was coming to the *Boogie Down Bronx/Condado De La Salsa.*

I explained how Serrano had sent the news release to the Cuban Interest Section in Washington and how they had also received it from the Cuban Mission to the United Nations, where our mutual friend, Franklin Flores, had probably sent it. We both marveled at how this could happen, and the next thing I remember saying was, "Thanks for getting me into this mess, and of course you're invited."

My next call was to Carlos Nazario, the president of the National Puerto Rican Business Council. I was trying to prepare my words, but then I remembered that Carlos and the Council would probably be looking at this as a blessing. My argument that the Cubans would now have a direct understanding of a Puerto Rican business organization in the United States was now a reality. Besides the NPRBC was a new organization that needed to be known; this dinner with Fidel was definitely going to put the National Puerto Rican Business Council on the map as the organization that invited Fidel Castro to the Bronx.

I called Carlos and told him how the press release had made it to Fidel's hands and what he had said about the invitation being the equivalent of getting a Nobel Prize. *"Dile a los hermanos puertorriqueños que estaré allí con ellos que para mi esto es como recibir un premio Nobel."* Carlos reacted much as David and I had, using a similar explicative, "Holy shit, Fidel is really coming." However, Carlos' remark was more like he was excited about what I had just shared with him rather than from fear or asking, "What have we done?"

I was relieved that Carlos responded so positively and pragmatically. He then asked me if I had called Jimmy Rodríguez regarding the fact that we were now going to have an event at the restaurant. I told him that Jimmy was next on my list of calls. We had already approved $500 for expenses, so we had a little working capital. All I had to do now was call Jimmy and tell him that we would be using the restaurant for a small private dinner. I ended the conversation with Carlos by telling him to start making a list of which members he wanted to invite to the private dinner. I asked him to remind those that he invited that this was an NPRBC event and that Fidel was our guest. Carlos understood and we agreed to meet and review the list and the details for the dinner.

Jimmy Rodríguez was rarely in the restaurant early, so I had a few hours to continue to plan the dinner. However, Serrano had called again and gave me a list of about twenty people that he wanted to invite. He also gave me the telephone numbers for the U.S. Secret Service and explained that they had reached out to him and indicated that they wanted to meet with the person organizing the event. I asked Serrano why the Secret Service wanted to meet with me. He explained that this was probably protocol since they were responsible for the safety and security of Fidel Castro while he was in New York City. I told Serrano that I still had a lot of work to do organizing the dinner and would not have time to meet with these security agents. Serrano insisted that I meet with them and that he would help by calling Jimmy Rodríguez for me and letting him know the dinner with Fidel at his restaurant was going to happen. In a way I was glad that Serrano volunteered to call Jimmy. I knew that if I called, he would remind me about what I had told him that, "This was is just a press release, Fidel is not really going to come" and probably raise all kinds of hell with me. I was used to this, as he and I were constantly debating, or play fighting. But I knew that on this one he would not make it easy on me.

I was not happy about meeting with the U.S. Secret Service. I had nothing to hide, but growing up in the South Bronx and being involved in serious leftist politics when I was younger, had left a bad taste in my mouth from past encounters with police and FBI agents. Coming from a revolutionary background, I was not exactly happy about having to meet with members of the U.S. Secret Service. Since my days of being a member of El Comité - MINP, I had worked to clean up my image as a leftist with U.S. security agencies like the FBI that had been on my case for years. During my brief period with the Young Lords and the years with El Comité – MINP, I had many negative experiences with the various security agencies. My phones had been tapped; I had been followed; I had been pulled off planes and harassed; and had experienced illegal searches in my apartment with fictitious warrants that were not for our apartment, but for some other address that was only shown after they had ransacked my room. Those days were over, as I had now worked at various levels of government — federal, state and city. In the latter two, I had worked with respectable elected officials, and I felt I had appeased "big brother," who no longer had any reason to watch me. I had gone through several security background checks and they were all fine. I believed I was now "clean" and not seen as a threatening radical. However, I was not comfortable with meeting any government security agents.

Little by little, this news release was having more and more of an impact on my personal life. I was now being directly affected by what was happening when a person like President Fidel Castro comes to your neighborhood, especially at your invitation. I figured that was how the U.S. State Department and the security agencies must have seen this and that was why they wanted to talk to me.

# FROM EVADING TO MEETING
## LAW ENFORCEMENT

I came to the conclusion that there was no way I could avoid meeting with the Secret Service. Although I began simply as the person organizing the writing of a news release, I had now become the organizer of an official event for one of the most controversial international figures, so I had to meet with the Secret Service. I was preparing myself mentally for a meeting where I was not the target of an investigation or of any harassment. But when the majority of your experiences with local and state police and federal agents have been negative, or even abusive, one tends to build up walls and avoid those meetings as much as possible. That's how I felt, and it still seemed strange to me to have the Secret Service ask to meet with me. Boy, was this going to be interesting.

# MY MEETING WITH THE U.S. SECRET SERVICE

I called the telephone number that Congressman Serrano had given me and spoke to an agent. I told him who I was and that I had been asked by Congressman Serrano to call them regarding the Castro visit. Apparently they knew all of this and had been expecting my call. We agreed to meet in a restaurant in midtown Manhattan. One thing I had learned in my more radical days was to always meet in a public place when you don't really trust the other party. I remember there were three agents. They were all males: two Anglos in their mid-forties and a younger one who stood out because he was sharply dressed and looked like he could have had a little Latino blood in him. He had a tinge of a tan, looking more like someone who had been cast for a role in a James Bond type of movie. I remember that my first thought was that he reminded me of the actor, Efrem Zimbalist, Jr. who had starring roles in the television series *77 Sunset Strip* and *The FBI.* He was the one that did most of the talking.

His first question to me was to ask me why was I doing this? I thought nothing of the question and answered it the same way I had answered many of my own friends and some family members who had asked me the same question. I explained the whole issue from my reaction to the mayor's disinviting Fidel Castro, to the decision to put out a news release, to the Congressman informing me that Fidel Castro was coming to the Bronx. Because the meeting had been arranged through Serrano's office, I felt I had more leverage and did not feel defensive like I usually did when talking with law enforcement agents. Then he and the other two agents began bombarding me from all sides about the impact the event could have. Was I sure that I wanted to be responsible for having such a meeting? Did I really think this through? It did not take me long to realize that despite their nice and caring - sounding tones, they were doing everything they could to scare me away from doing what I was doing.

# SECRET SERVICE VS. ACTIVIST

I patiently listened to all three agents giving advice and expressing their concerns for me. As they spoke, I would shake my head up in and down every so often as though I was agreeing with what they were saying. The fact was that much of what they were saying was true. For one, I really had no idea what I was getting into with this dinner. I for one never planned on Fidel attending an event that was only mentioned in a news release. Nor did I have any experience planning an event for a world leader. Sure, I had planned several luncheons for athletes and dinners and dances for community and political organizations, but those events were child's play compared to what I was organizing now. But despite these agents' best efforts to get me to cancel the event, that possibility was totally out of the question. This dinner was now a done deal. Congressman Serrano, Carlos Nazario and I had already spoken and this dinner was a go.

I thanked them for their advice, but told them that the dinner was not going to be cancelled.

They looked at each other somewhat confused; perhaps they thought they would have been able to scare the living daylights out of this young Puerto Rican from the South Bronx. They had probably read my profile and knew that I was beginning to move away from radical politics to becoming more involved with community organizing and a progressive democratic agenda. They also knew that I was beginning to test the waters of private business and they were prepared to play on all of those leads. "This could really hurt your chances of moving up on any future corporate, or governmental career", I remember one of them saying. However, I stood my ground and they then switched to their Plan B. And I was ready.

This one was even more creative. They went from the personal and trying to get me to cancel the event to going back into their comfort zone, by trying to get me to move the event from the South Bronx to Manhattan.

Though I was open to the idea of listening to suggestions, I was taken for a loop on this one. Moving the event from the Bronx to Manhattan? No way. We were all Bronxites and Manhattan was not going to be an option. I asked them why they wanted us to change locations. They explained that the security details for Fidel Castro were quite extensive and that they were much better suited to protect him in Manhattan where they had better resources than in the South Bronx.

I could hardly believe what they were admitting. They were acknowledging that they had no control if the event was held in the Bronx. Wow! I always knew that our borough was one of the most neglected, but now I saw that we were so neglected that even the highest level of U.S. law enforcement had no resources in the borough. I also could not help but smile as they were telling me this and thinking, could it be possible that even the Secret Service is afraid of coming up to the Bronx?

Now I felt that the table had turned and I had the power of controlling them as opposed to them trying to control me. Personally, I was beginning to enjoy this game of words and action. I had never been in a situation with any law enforcement agency where I felt I could actually talk to them as equals. I always felt like a victim in my other encounters with police, detectives, immigration agents, the border patrol, or the FBI. However, I did not feel like that now. In this meeting in a restaurant in Manhattan, I was not feeling like a victim. The wheels had turned and it was the Secret Service who was on the defensive, not me. For whatever reason they did not want the event to take place, and they especially did not want it to take place in the Bronx. Perhaps it was stressful enough to have to protect Fidel Castro in New York City, but to have to protect him in the South Bronx was definitely not something they had anticipated when they first got this assignment.[x] For the first time, as a South Bronx-raised Puerto Rican I felt like I was on an equal footing with these agents working for one of the highest levels of security in the country. Man, that felt good.

I listened attentively as they continued giving me the reasons that they wanted me to move the dinner to Manhattan. I wish I could have taken a picture of their faces when I told them that unfortunately, the dinner could not be moved. For one, we did not have enough time to find a new location (although I thought they would have been more than willing to find us a restaurant, or other location). But the fact was that if they did not feel comfortable in the Bronx, I did not feel comfortable in Manhattan. Obviously they were disappointed, they expressed that to me in their tone and insinuating that I was not cooperating in a way that would guarantee the best security for President Fidel Castro. They were making me feel that if something did go wrong in the Bronx, I would be held responsible. Though I felt a lot of pressure at that moment, I still did not budge and maintained my position that the dinner had to take place in our home, the Bronx. They then proceeded to bombard me with a list of demands that had to be met no later than 24 hours prior to the dinner. Considering that the dinner was on Monday night and we were meeting Saturday, that did not give us much leeway. They wanted the name, address, social security number, date and place of birth, and contact information for each person attending the dinner. I told them that they would have the information, and departed thinking of the additional workload that had just been added to my schedule. The rest of this Saturday and Sunday was definitely going to be a heavy workday. This was not going to be a restful weekend.

# FEELING GOOD AFTER MEETING
## U.S. SECRET SERVICE

Still, I felt good after my meeting with the Secret Service agents. It was the first time I had had dealings with a U.S. law enforcement agency that I felt I had come out on top. It was a strange feeling. Since coming to the United States from Puerto Rico, neither I, nor my family had ever been made to feel like what we were — U.S. citizens. It was always "them and us." "Them" were those people outside my world of a Puerto Rican living in the South Bronx. Yet we were all American citizens. But in all my past encounters, including this latest one with the Secret Service, I was never made to feel if I was part of this nation. My experience growing up in the South Bronx was that I was always made to feel as if I was a second-class citizen, an immigrant even though I was born a U.S. citizen. But after my meeting with the agents, not only did I feel as if I had held my own, somehow I felt I had won. The dinner was not going to be cancelled, and we were not going to move the location of the dinner from our comfort zone in the South Bronx to their comfort zone in Manhattan.

The subway ride back to the Bronx from Manhattan was quite pleasant. I was oblivious to the panhandlers and pushing crowds of the subway mayhem riding the Lexington Avenue train uptown. I had a Kool-Aid smile all the way back to the office.

When I returned to the office Kimberly asked me how the meeting went. I told her it went well and I believe I was still smiling ear to ear. I sat down in my cube ready to make a few calls and share the experience I had just had with the U.S. Secret Service with several of my closest friends. Unfortunately, that was not to be. One of the first calls I received was from Serrano who wanted to add more names to the guest list for the private dinner that was now becoming more public as the hours ticked by. The list of guests had already surpassed the limit of perhaps 25-30 that I had originally set. This call from Serrano was to add some additional names as well as to tell me that he received a call from the Cuban Mission and that their security detail also wanted to meet with me.

I already knew the importance of having to meet with the Cubans so I did not ask Serrano if this was really necessary as I had about the meeting with the U.S. Secret Service. I was sure the Cubans were more concerned with Fidel's safety than anyone else and that was a top priority for me now as well after seeing how concerned the U.S. Secret Service was about holding our event in the Bronx. It was public knowledge that the CIA and some of their operatives had been involved in many assassination attempts against the Cuban leader for years after the triumph of the 1959 Cuban revolution, and this was reason enough for the Cuban secret service to be preoccupied. So I noted the telephone number down and forgot about calling my family and close friends. I did however tell Serrano of all the information that we now had to provide to the U.S. Secret Service for all guests – those who had already been invited, and those whose invitations were still to come.

I wanted to get this next meeting with the Cuban security detail and others related to the dinner over with as soon as possible. The dinner was two days away and we had limited time. I needed to spend more time in my office to coordinate the growing guest list and coordinate other logistical issues related to the dinner that included providing all the information that the secret service had requested for every guest attending. Not to mention my own businesses that I had been neglecting. This Fidel Castro visit was now taking up all of my time. After Serrano's phone call, I immediately called the number for the Cuban Secret Service.

Unlike the first call to the U.S. Secret Service, on this call we only spoke in Spanish. It felt a little odd speaking to the security detail from another country about the security of their leader. The difference was that in this phone conversation, I did not have the apprehensions I had when I called the U.S. Secret Service. The person I was speaking to already knew who I was and asked if we could meet soon, like later that afternoon or early evening. I had just returned from Manhattan and was not excited about the idea of returning for another meeting in midtown. I explained that I had already met with the U.S. Secret Service. I told him that we met in a Manhattan restaurant and the Cuban agent stated that they could do the same. I knew that this was important, so I agreed to meet in two hours at a diner not far from the Cuban mission on 38th Street and Lexington Avenue. We described ourselves so we could recognize each other in the restaurant. I made it easy for them and told them that I would be wearing a Latino Sports baseball cap.

# MEETING WITH THE CUBAN SECRET SERVICE

I went to the designated diner as agreed and looked around to see if I saw the Cuban agents. I did not know who I was looking for, but I thought that I would probably be able to recognize them, if for no other reason than they might look Caribbean, perhaps with a little more color than the majority of the patrons in the restaurant. However, I knew that a Caribbean look, or color is not a guarantee, my mother was a pure Puerto Rican from the island, who passed for Italian many times in New York, because she was light-skinned, and had freckles with hazel eyes. I Looked and did not identify anyone, so I took a seat at a booth facing the door. This way I could see everyone entering the restaurant.

I imagined that there must have been U.S. agents following and tracking these Cuban agents, just as they were also probably tracking me. I also suspected that the U.S. Secret Service was keeping tabs on me. I could not help but think that all the time and energy that I had invested in leaving my radical past behind, was quickly going out the window. I no longer wanted to appear as a threat to the State and I wanted to leave behind the life that kept me constantly looking over my shoulder, with all the accompanying surveillance and harassment. Yet, here I was deeper into politics than I wished or cared to be. A meeting with top security agents for both the United States and Cuba, a foreign country that the U.S. considered an enemy, was definitely going to put me back into the spotlight and could once again cause the authorities to target me. I could not help but think that after these meetings with the secret services of both countries combined with the fact that Fidel Castro was actually going to come to the Bronx, I would now probably be considered more of a threat than in the decades past. Life does have interesting turns. I just thought about that old street saying, "Life's a bitch and then you die."

The two Cubans finally arrived; they identified me at the booth where I was sitting because my black cap with the "Latino Sports" logo on it was hard to miss. I was sitting facing the restaurant door and the fact that I was probably the only Latino-looking man in the restaurant also helped.

This meeting had a long lasting visual effect on my mind. The early evening had turned cloudy and the two Cuban agents that approached appeared to be wearing identical beige trench coats, of the type that you see in the movies with the belt at the waist. I could not help but wonder, how I got myself in this situation that had all the markings of an "*I Spy*" movie.

They sat down across from me and introduced themselves. After the basic formalities, they asked me about the upcoming Bronx dinner with their Commander in Chief. They asked about the agenda for the evening. They asked about the location of the restaurant, its owner, who we were inviting and the number of guests. I answered their questions as best as I could, but could not tell them how many people were coming because the list was still being put together, even as we spoke, and I did not have an accurate count. They also asked me about the meeting I had with the U.S. Secret Service agents; the questions they had and the information they wanted. I found the Cuban agents more pleasant, with no demands. Nor did they make any effort to try and persuade me to see things their way. They were very cordial and just asked me to send them copies of everything that I was sending to the U.S. Secret Service. This meeting was quick and to the point. It lasted less than half the time of the meeting I had with their U.S. counterparts. They excused themselves and left. I was impressed that they did not ask me questions about the security of the Bronx, as I was sure they too had heard negative things about the borough. But then I thought that agents assigned to protect Fidel Castro had to be seasoned veterans who could handle any location. I remained watching them as they left and tried to catch the eye of any of the customers scoping them out as they exited. After these two meetings, I was beginning to recall a lot of the old security training I had learned from my days in the movement and was instinctively applying it again.

As I headed back to the Bronx, my second subway ride uptown in a day, I started to once again think about the situation. I had just finished meeting with Cuban agents a few blocks from the Cuban Mission to the United Nations, a place that I had visited perhaps three or four times in over 30 years. The Cuban Mission had held numerous receptions honoring special days and events of the Cuban revolution, exclusively for people who had direct contacts with the Cubans; members of the U.S. Communist Party, progressive scholars and other individuals on the left, usually who held leadership positions. I was never a member of any of those organizations, nor was I a leader during my radical days. I was always interested in attending events and going inside the Cuban mission, mostly out of curiosity. I had been to Cuba in 1978 to attend the International World Youth Festival in Havana. Since my return from that festival, I had a better understanding of Cuba, but never followed up, or got involved with any of the "above ground" leftist organizations that were doing work with Cuba and were frequently invited to the Cuban Mission. The Youth Festival was a great opportunity to meet other young people and learn about the struggles taking place in different communities throughout the world. When I returned from that festival, I realized that I needed to spend more time organizing in my own community in the South Bronx. So here I was now, 17 years later, meeting with Cuban agents attached to that mission a few blocks away.

On that subway ride home, I started to once again think about many things. I was now seeing the politics of what we were doing, beyond our reaction to a mayor's insult. I thought about the hard times I had growing up in the South Bronx and constantly being made to feel like a second-class citizen. I remember later in college learning about Cuba and the peoples' struggle to maintain their revolution. I remembered returning from that trip to the International World Youth Festival in Havana and wondered if that was how the universe worked — by bringing me to this point in my life where I was spearheading a move to assure that the Cuban leader, Fidel Castro, and the Cuban people get the respect that they deserve?

I could not help but feel proud knowing that Cuba, a small nation when compared to the United States, had defied the U.S. attempts to destroy its revolution on so many occasions. Though I did not understand all the politics of the time affecting the island, I felt a bond. It was in part knowing that this island, close to my island of birth, Puerto Rico, with a similar flag and a common language, had stood up to mighty "Uncle Sam." It was as if Cuba was a lifeline for me. It made me believe that I, too, could stand up to the many abuses I had experienced.

I also remembered that during my college days my closest contact with revolutionary Cubans was when I attended events organized by Casa De Las Americas, at their center on 14th Street in Manhattan. The organization would always sponsor dances and cultural events, often for the entire family, in support of the Cuban revolution.

I attended many events at Casa De Las Américas with my family. I remember that was the only place that you could have an intelligent conversation with Cuban old timers who had always supported, or actually been involved in the Cuban revolution. They also had old copies of the Cuban newspaper, *Granma,* and several magazines from Cuba. I used to like reading them and sharing them with my father who was a socialist at heart from his days working in the cane fields of Puerto Rico and who was an admirer of Dr. Pedro Albizu Campos, president of the Nationalist Party and leader of the Puerto Rican independence movement. That meeting with the Cuban security detail made me think and remember a lot more about Cuba and myself than I would have imagined.  Unlike the meeting with the U.S. Secret Service agents, where I was on the defensive, I went into my meeting with the Cubans feeling comfortable and with an open mind, and left with a strengthened commitment to our mutual struggle for respect and self determination.

# MY CONCERN WITH SECURITY FOR FIDEL

That subway ride uptown back to my office seemed longer than ever and it was because my mind kept wandering. When I arrived at my office, I began to think about security for Fidel Castro. The fact that the U.S. Secret Service agents had tried to make me feel that I was making it difficult for them to protect President Castro by not canceling, or moving the event to Manhattan, kept playing itself over and over in my mind. Could something happen? If something did happen would it be my fault for not moving the event to a Manhattan location? Would I ever forgive myself if something did happen? Could forces at play use this impromptu event in the Bronx as a cover to plan something against President Castro? My head was spinning and I kept thinking of the serious meetings I had with agents from both countries regarding President Castro's security. The fact that I was a key player in terms of arranging security in the eyes of the agents from both countries did not make me feel any more comfortable.

So I began to seriously think about the issue of security. When I was involved with leftist movements, I was always part of some type of security detail, perhaps because of my early martial arts training and the fact that I taught martial arts to members of security details and to youth in the community. When I was in my senior year at Lehman College, we practically paralyzed the college with one of the most successful student takeovers in Lehman college history with a plan I developed. I was also involved with many security details that required strategy, such as securing places for forums and outdoor festivals. I was always "volunteered" to serve on the security detail for visiting revolutionaries from Latin America and for Puerto Rican patriot, Lolita Lebrón when she was released after serving 25 years in a federal prison. Thus, I knew enough about security to start thinking about my own possible security plan for Fidel Castro.

I also kept thinking about the comment made by the U.S. secret service agent about "the seriousness of securing the site for Fidel Castro." That comment made me think that perhaps this event could be used as a possible site for staging something against the Cuban leader. It was in the Bronx, an unfamiliar place for the U.S. Secret Service, which made them oppose the Bronx as a location. Our dinner was also an unexpected event that was not on any pre-planned agenda from either the Cubans or American side when they first reviewed all the protocols for Fidel's visit. All of this was going through my mind when I decided that aside from what both the U.S. and Cuban security teams would be doing, we had to have our own security. I began to go back to my old days of street survival — "only trust yourself and your closest people."

# PLANNING OUR OWN SECURITY

Since I had not been involved in any security details with the left for some time, and I no longer had contact with most of the brothers and sisters that I had worked with routinely before, I had to think of alternatives. I still had many street contacts in the South Bronx, but for this I needed more than numbers and muscle. When we built the National Puerto Rican Business Council we came across a variety of Puerto Rican businessmen and women. Many were already established in solid businesses; others like myself had start-ups and were learning to network with others for the first time. The NPRBC provided an excellent opportunity for us to do this. That is how I met and became friends with, Jerry "Fast Feet" Fontanez, a martial artist who was ranked as the number one kickboxing champion in the world. Because of my martial arts background, Jerry and I had become close friends. Jerry had several *dojos* and I had frequented the one in the Bronx several times when he held several of his own tournaments.

I immediately thought of Jerry to be part of my own internal security inside Jimmy's restaurant on the night of the dinner. I knew that U.S. and Cuban secret service agents would be there in force to protect Fidel. But my untrusting mind kept worrying that something, anything, could happen, so I wanted to make sure that I had people who I could count on just in case something did occur. I also thought about my meeting with the U.S. secret service agents that, in my opinion, did not go well. I sensed their frustration with me for not canceling the event, or at least moving it to another location. That encounter did not reassure me or make me feel any safer.

Reverting in my mind to my activist days, I started thinking about securing the restaurant. I knew Jimmy's Bronx Café well since I had had many Latino Sports baseball award luncheons there with some of the top Latino athletes. I had also been visiting the site with the owner, Jimmy Rodríquez from its earliest days, when it was still under construction. In those early years, I had been helping Jimmy promote, both the original restaurant, Mariscos Del Caribe on Webster Avenue, and what was then the soon-to-be-built massive restaurant and catering hall, Jimmy's Bronx Café. Jimmy was very proud of this project, as it was his biggest, and one that would be exclusively developed and owned by him, unlike Mariscos Del Caribe on Webster Avenue, started by his father. A Puerto Rican-owned upscale restaurant and catering facility with the best Caribbean cuisine would be a first for the Bronx and Jimmy wanted to show it to as many of his friends and contacts as possible. Therefore, every time I visited him at Mariscos Del Caribe on Webster Avenue he would whisk me over to Fordham Road to see the development and construction details of the new massive, "coming soon," Jimmy's Bronx Café.

My knowledge of the restaurant and its overall space made it easy for me to think about a security plan for Fidel's visit. My concern was basically focused on the actual catering hall, the place where the dinner would take place, and not the overall building and surrounding area. I knew that the outside areas and the actual building were going to be secured by the secret service and I was sure that they were not going to allow any of us, or our internal security, to have any access to their locations. So I just focused on a plan for the entrance to the restaurant and the room where the dinner was to take place.

My mind was focused just on security when my daughter Kimberly reminded me that there were still many other things to think about in regards to the dinner. She approached me about a number of issues, including the names of more guests to invite who had been suggested by Congressman Serrano, and a slew of messages, requiring a response. I remember putting both my hands up and telling her that I needed to make an important call first before sitting down with her as I did not want to get sidetracked from the issue of security.

I immediately called Jerry Fontanez to tell him about the dinner, my experience with the U.S. and Cuban secret service agents, and the reason I needed his help. Jerry might have not known all of the political ramifications of this dinner for Fidel Castro, nor was he up to date on the politics of Cuba, but his response was as reassuring and solid as any loyal and tested leftist veteran that I had worked with. He said, "I got you." That put another Kool Aid smile on my face, knowing that I had friends like Jerry who did not need a lot of information, details, or convincing to get on board. If he could help, he was down for whatever. That type of loyalty was something that had been lacking in my new endeavors in community politics and business development, so it was quite refreshing to know that our community still had individuals like Jerry in the mix.

When we got down to the details I told Jerry that I might need about five or six of his top black belts to help secure a dining hall and to help with general security, I also told him that at least one of the security personnel had to be a female. My plan was simple. I wanted Jerry to dress up his people, scatter them in the room, and let them mingle with the dinner guests. I instructed Jerry on what to do if for whatever reason an instigator, agent or anyone who wanted to disrupt, or worse, hurt Fidel got through the U.S. and Cuban security teams. I told him I wanted him and his security people to focus on that individual and isolate him or her from the crowd and hold them for the Secret Service to handle, or if they were not available, for him to handle. I loved his response: "No problem, I got you."

Now I was beginning to feel a little more in control of this dinner that was not supposed to happen and that was being organized in just 72 hours. Though I really did not know how, or when, or if we would need to use our own security, I did feel much better knowing that we would have a security detail inside the dinner and someone like Jerry who I could count on, someone who I knew and trusted.

# NEEDING MORE HELP

When I finished handling the security issue, I got back to Kimberly's messages. We had approximately two days to work out any additional details before Fidel's visit. The location was set. I had already met with the secrets services of both the Cuban and U.S. governments, and knew what they wanted. I took care of that and added another layer of security with people who would only respond to us, and not to any government agency, whether American or Cuban. Both National Puerto Rican Business Council President Carlos Nazario and Congressman Serrano's office were up to date and providing all the information needed for the Secret Service. Now my attention focused on the names on the growing guest list. I had wanted to keep the dinner small to appease the Congressman's concern of any possible disruptions and because of my own belief that a small dinner would be easier to organize. By now I realized why Kimberly was trying to get my attention when I first returned to the office. The guest list had substantially grown to about 300 people. Whatever concern Congressman Serrano might have had at first was obviously no longer a problem, as the majority of the proposed guests were coming from him. The NPRBC and my list were small and had already been reviewed and processed, but every time we received a new name, we had to do the whole routine of obtaining and checking the information required before sending it first to the U.S. Secret Service and then another copy of the information to the Cubans. It seemed that Serrano's office was calling every few hours to add additional names, which was frustrating Kimberly.

I realized that to review all the information we had to submit to the secret services of both countries, plus all the other ancillary items like preparing an agenda, decorations, menu, seating arrangements and our own internal security, had become way too much for Kimberly and I to handle. Also the growing list of guests was beginning to read like the "Who's Who of the Puerto Rican Community." The list included executives, administrators, elected officials, and names that I knew like City Councilman José Rivera, Congresswoman Nydia Velasquez, Dr. Ricardo Fernández, President of Lehman College, musicians like Willie Colón, former light heavyweight boxing champion and established writer, José "Chegüí" Torres, the great, pianist, arranger and composer Chucho Valdez Sr., and his bass player, Carlos Emilio Morales. I recognized those two Cuban names as I had just bought this incredible album of a new jazz group in Cuba, *Irakere*. Apparently these two musicians from this group were visiting New York and they somehow made it to our VIP list.

This event had turned into the most important and popular event in the Puerto Rican/Latino community and it seemed many more people than any of us imagined wanted to come. It was the hottest ticket in New York. Upon perusing the list I saw that these were not just progressives, but people from all walks of life and from all over the city.

I suspected that this was going to be worse than planning a wedding between warring families. I knew that Kimberly and I needed help.

I called Serrano and expressed my concern with the ever-growing list that was mainly being generated by his office. I told him he needed to stop inviting people and sending us names every couple of hours, because each time he did this, we had to redo the master list and verify all the information that the Secret Service had requested. I reminded him that this small private dinner had now turned into a major banquet with more than 300 attendees and a list that was still growing. I also told him it was becoming too difficult to handle and that we still had many logistical things to arrange and less than 72 hours in which to do it. I suggested that he assign some of his staff to help. He expressed concerns about that and suggested that I get additional help from elsewhere. He recommended Gerson Borrero, the *El Diario* newspaper reporter to whom he had most likely leaked the information about the dinner before we had sent out the news release. I rejected his name simply because Gerson was a reporter and I felt we needed top secrecy with everything we were doing. The less information people had about the details of the event, the better. I did not believe that Gerson would be able to separate himself from his role as a reporter for *El Diario* to work on a high-level event where secrecy was critical.

I recommended Mickey Melendez, a former member of the Young Lords Party, who had a good reputation within leftist and progressive circles in the city. After I left the Young Lords, I had worked on several coalition projects representing El Comité – MINP where Mickey had also worked. Serrano knew Mickey and agreed that he was a good choice.

I had already called my friend Franklin Flores; I had been talking to him quite frequently about the event, even before President Castro accepted. Franklin knew the Cuban community and many people in the Cuban Mission to the United Nations quite well. Many might have confused Franklin for a Cuban because he did so much work on Cuban causes, but I knew him as a staunch Puerto Rican. Franklin and his wife Nancy (she's Cuban) had a close association and had done a lot of work with *Casa De Las Américas*, the Cuban cultural center in New York. I had known Franklin for quite some time as he was one of my early recruits to the carpenters union apprenticeship program when I was working for the federally-funded Recruitment and Training Program (RTP), a program that funded us to recruit and place minorities and women into the hard-to-get-into trade unions. I was director of the RTP office in Harlem in the mid- 1970s, where I met and recruited Franklin. He was one of our success stories completing the application and training process and eventually becoming an apprentice and then a journeyman with the union.

Franklin was a trusted and reliable friend. He also had a better command of the Spanish language than any of us — Mickey, Kimberly, or myself. When I had asked Franklin to help, he did not hesitate to join me in helping to organize the logistics of the event. The same was true when I called Mickey.

Serrano agreed to stop inviting people to the dinner. He explained that now people who would not even talk to him before, were calling to try and get an invitation. As an elected official, I imagined Serrano was in heaven and in a unique position for a politician. When he first learned that Fidel had accepted the invitation (that was not really an invitation, but a news release), he was practically cursing me. He was concerned about the political ramifications of potential protests and attacks on his office by right-wing sectors within our community and the extreme anti-Castro Cuban community who lived across the river in New Jersey. But now Serrano must have felt exhilarated as the man who held the cards as to who could be invited to the most popular event in our community. These were not poor people calling his office for a job, a letter of recommendation, help with Section Eight housing, or immigration. His office was now being inundated with calls from professionals, business people and politicians asking, perhaps begging, for a chance to see President Fidel Castro in person. The majority of those people, like many of my non-leftist friends, did not support the Cuban Revolution, or Fidel Castro. Nevertheless, they all wanted a chance to see the Cuban leader who had probably given the United States government more grief than any other Latin American leader in history. They all wanted a chance to see Fidel Castro, one of the most popular and controversial figures of the time. President Fidel Castro was coming to the Bronx and we had made Congressman José Serrano the gatekeeper. I knew he was in his glory so I went along with his growing list and had put an imaginary number in my mind of no more than 350 people, the capacity of the banquet hall at Jimmy's Bronx Café. I had to take into account all the other people invited, our internal security, my personal contacts, family members, and Franklin's list that had been generated by the Cuban mission. There was also the issue of the media, even though I still was not too clear how we were going to handle the increasingly interested and ever-growing press corps.

# GETTING CLOSER TO D DAY –
# DISCUSSING LOGISTICS

Mickey, Franklin and I met Sunday morning in my office to discuss the details of the dinner. We had approximately 32 hours to put together an agenda and work on the seating plan. We also had about another eight hours to go over the VIP guest list one last time, add any new guests that we each had and have a complete and final list to send over to the U.S. Secret Service. Since my initial meeting with the Secret Service was not the most cordial, I did not want to give them any excuse to blame me for any problems with guests. They requested a complete and final list no later than 24 hours prior to the dinner, which meant by 6 p.m. Sunday, and I was going to comply.

Upon reviewing the guest list and adding names of our own last-minute guests, we saw that we now had over 300 people. We agreed that we had to close the list within the next few hours. That was my signal to reach out to both, Carlos Nazario and Congressman José Serrano and tell them that the cutoff time to propose additional names for the guest list was approaching, reminding them of the deadline imposed by the Secret Service. In other words, I let them know I would be submitting a final list of names by early evening.

Carlos was on point and told me that he had already submitted all guest names from the National Puerto Rican Business Council and that he had no additional names to submit. Congressman Serrano said he still had a few more names he wanted to review and said he would get back to me before the deadline. I told him that I had to turn in the list by 5 p.m., taking one hour off our deadline, so we would have a one-hour leeway.

# WORKING OUT THE PROGRAM

After working on the list and the seating arrangements we began to work on the agenda for the event. There had to be a welcome, a presentation of the event and then the introduction of President Fidel Castro. We had received numerous requests from people who wanted to make a special presentation, perform, or give President Castro a gift, but we decided that none of that was going to happen. We wanted to keep the event as simple and streamlined as possible. We also wanted to give it a very professional appearance with clockwork precision, although with a touch of our Puerto Rican/Latino culture. And of course the event had to have a politically progressive message. It was a tall order, but not impossible for three radical veterans. We discussed this at length since we had to make sure that we were keeping the event short and allow the bulk of the time to be given over for Fidel's presentation, since we knew Fidel's presentations were usually not short, and we wanted to allow the most time for him.

# PLANNING THE AGENDA

We agreed that there should be three short presentations. The first was going to be a welcome address from the sponsoring organization, to be done by Carlos Nazario, president of the National Puerto Rican Business Council. We agreed that Carlos would then introduce me and that I would explain why we were holding the dinner and how it came to be. We wanted to make sure that everyone present knew how Mayor Giuliani had disrespected us and the international community by disinviting President Fidel Castro from the dinner he had organized for visiting world leaders. I knew that not everyone that was invited was sympathetic to the Cuban revolution, but they agreed that the mayor was wrong in snubbing President Fidel Castro. Mickey and Franklin also agreed that the purpose of the dinner needed to be specified in my presentation, making it necessary for my presentation to be a little longer than the welcome. We agreed that Congressman Serrano would be the appropriate person to introduce President Fidel Castro and that his presentation could be longer than mine. But once we got the agenda done, we started to think it was a bit bland, and a bit too business-like and formal. We thought it needed some warmth and some life before getting to the "seriousness" of the night's main presentation. Franklin suggested that we have some of our children present Fidel with gifts. We thought this was a good idea. We could have the children present the gifts to Fidel right after Serrano introduced him, but just before Fidel would begin his presentation. However, although we thought this was a good idea, it also opened up a discussion on the possible consequences that being up on stage and being photographed with Fidel Castro could mean for that young person. How might that affect them for the rest of their lives? Would they be put on a government watch list? Would that label them as potential radicals who needed to be under constant surveillance? Definitely we would be exposing them to attention from the state. We grappled with these questions longer than it took us to do the entire agenda. We finally agreed that it was not fair to choose young children, and that it was better to select teenagers who were old enough for us to speak with so we could explain the ramifications of being in the spotlight by presenting Fidel Castro with a gift. We also had to speak to their parents, get their permission and also make them aware of what this might mean for them and their child. We narrowed down our list of teens to a very short one and to no one's surprise it was our own children who we had placed on the list. Franklin spoke with his wife, Nancy, about having their then 10-year-old daughter, Elena, present Fidel with a bouquet of flowers, which we agreed would be white roses.

We began to think about what other gifts we might give to a world leader like Fidel Castro. I remembered that I had compiled a list of the people who had contacted us to ask if they could give Fidel a gift. I had their names and the gifts that they wanted to give. I reviewed the list and found something that was appropriate. A local businessman named Dante, whose office was across the street from mine and who made trophies, plaques, boxing robes, and equipment had offered to give Fidel a huge boxing glove with the words written on it: "FIDEL # 1." We all liked the idea of the glove and decided it would be best if a young man gave that gift to Fidel. We thought about my youngest, my son Julio Antonio Pabón, who was 15 at the time. I told them that while I was all for the idea, I had to speak to both Julio Antonio and to his mother before making a commitment. I personally had no problem with Julio Antonio's participation, as I already believed that all the members of my family were on some government list anyway. Julio's mother, Elizabeth Figueroa, and

I, had been members of El Comité – MINP (*Movimiento de Izquierda Nacional Puertorriqueño*) a political organization fighting for social rights here and for the liberation of Puerto Rico since we were in college. We had both been to Cuba. She had gone in 1977, as a member of the *Venceremos* Brigade, an organization that sent groups of young people to Cuba every year to help with the construction or development of a variety of projects. The *Brigadistas* spent approximately one month in Cuba, working, on a project for about two weeks and then touring the island and learning about the Cuban revolution for the next two weeks.

I had gone to Cuba in 1978 to attend the International World Festival of Youth and Students, an event organized since 1947, by the World Federation of Democratic Youth (WFDY) and the International Union of Students. I figured if both of us had been to Cuba, the chances of our family not being on some government watch list were quite slim. Therefore, if Julio Antonio agreed to do it we had no problems in him being one of those giving a gift to Fidel. So we had two gifts for Fidel and two youths to present the gifts.

Then I thought that this could be a great opportunity for my startup, Latino Sports. I had a line of clothing apparel in Latino Sports that I was beginning to market. What if I could get Fidel Castro to wear one of my hats? The publicity could be great and though I knew that it would not sell in Miami, or Union City, New Jersey, I did not care as I was only thinking about our local community and perhaps Puerto Rico at the time. We discussed it and both Franklin and Mickey reminded me of the possible repercussions, and reminded me that the idea could also backfire and my company could be boycotted by conservative sectors. But my mind was set. I always thought that in business any publicity is better than no publicity. Now we needed a third youth to give Fidel the hats. The first two youths were easy since they were our children, but we couldn't think of a third child who could present Fidel with a gift. We were stuck for a while on who to call. So we moved on with planning the dinner.

At some point during that meeting, my associate, Susana Rios who was working with me in my interpreting business, Morivivi Language Services, walked into the office to pick up and review some interpreting assignment schedules for the week. By now, just a day away from the event, I had been neglecting all of my other work. Susana Rios was a strict "by the book" professional who was an excellent manager, scheduling interpreters for Morivivi. Apparently, she was having a problem getting through to me on some issues related to Morivivi, so she decided to walk over to the office to talk to me personally. When she walked in, Mickey, Franklin and I were gathered around my conference table. Susana thought that she was disturbing an important meeting and waved herself away. I saw her and immediately thought of the third child.

Susana Rios and I had been working together for several years, and as a result we got to know each other's families quite well. Susana was from Chile and she had a pretty open mind regarding Cuba and Fidel. Her family had been living in Chile when the CIA helped organize the coup against the democratically elected socialist President Salvador Allende. Susana's family had endured serious hardships under dictator Augusto Pinochet. So I knew that she might be open to the idea. Susana had three daughters and I thought one of them would be perfect. I called her back to the conference room and told her what we were working on and what we were planning. She had no problems and she volunteered her youngest daughter, Vanessa Ramos. Perfect!

The last item left was my presentation, which we had decided would be the one that would explain, define, educate and motivate. We wanted Fidel and the Cubans to know who we were— Puerto Ricans/Latinos in New York who were not part of any revolutionary party, or organization, but who were proud of being Latino and who demanded respect for ourselves, our community and our guest from Cuba. I would then present Congressman Serrano, who would introduce Fidel Castro. I had my work cut out for me. I had written and helped write several speeches for elected officials, but I never wrote one for myself, as I would always speak from my heart with just a few notes.

However, Mickey and Franklin urged me to write a speech and have it ready by that evening, or at the latest the next morning, so that Franklin could translate it to Spanish. Though I speak Spanish, English is my dominant language and if I was to deliver a speech in Spanish, which was not my forte, I had to practice, something I rarely did for a speech.

I took the suggestions made by Franklin and Mickey and tried to get lost in my office of seven "cubes" and one conference room, but the cubes were not private, making it hard to be alone. With just one more day to go before the big event that had now taken over my entire life, I was under pressure to hurry up and write the speech, get it translated and read it a few times.

Franklin Flores and Julio Pabón working on the Spanish
translation of Julio's speech (Photo Personal Archives)

I kept thinking that after this last night, the big event would be just hours away. I believed that after this night all of the major work and frustrations would be over, and that all we still needed to do was review logistics, follow up with what we had planned, review the guest list one final time, and hope that there were no last minute changes or additions. I did not want the Secret Service rejecting any of the names already submitted, or asking for additional details about any of the guests, as they had already done in a few instances, sending some names back for further clarification. We had a good team. Mickey, Franklin, and Kimberly each had their work cut out and did it to precision. I wanted to make sure that everything would go smoothly the next day so that my life could return to normal after the event. Boy, was I wrong.

# DAY BEFORE BIG EVENT

I could not believe that in less than 24 hours this event that had taken over so much of my personal and business life, was about to take place. The days and hours had flown by.

I had to call Jimmy Rodríguez to review details and give him a final head count for the dinner. I also needed to call Carlos Nazario and José Serrano and go over the logistics and the agenda with them one last time. I also had to call Jerry Fontanez, my in-house security chief whose role I had kept a secret from everyone except the people working closest with me — Mickey, Franklin and Kimberly.

If necessary, Mickey, Franklin, Kimberly, and I had scheduled a meeting early the next day to review the agenda and seating plan one last time and go over any last minutes details. But still I had to work on my speech. I had spent some time while in the office during sporadic breaks to jot down a few notes. I had thought a lot about it and kind of had it all in my head, but I needed some time to write. I tried writing it in the office during breaks but it was almost impossible. My head was still spinning from everything that was going on, making it difficult for me to concentrate and sit quietly somewhere to write. However, I knew that I had to have it ready for Franklin by evening so he could translate it. I set aside some time in the late afternoon.

It reminded me of my college days when I had deadlines for my term papers, but always waited until the last minute to write them. I seem to always write best when I was under pressure.

By early evening I had finished the draft of my presentation and sent it to Franklin. I titled it, *Los Atrevidos* " (the daring ones). I wanted Fidel and the Cuban entourage to learn a little about the Puerto Rican community in the Bronx who had planned and organized the event. I also wanted them to know a little of the history of how we, the sons and daughters of that great Puerto Rican migration of the 1950s, had survived discrimination and many abuses in this cement jungle of New York we call home to become a growing power in the city and particularly the Bronx. I knew that Fidel had visited New York twice before. His second visit in 1960, right after the triumph of the revolution, probably had the most impact. Fidel had come to the United States to address the United Nations and he had stayed in the Teresa Hotel in Harlem (now the Teresa Towers, an office building). So Fidel had demonstrated his very close affinity to the African-American community. However, I was sure that Fidel had never visited the Bronx, the borough with the largest Puerto Rican/Latino population in the city. I wanted Fidel to remember this visit and know that the Bronx, particularly, the South Bronx had stood up for a world leader to show respect. I also wanted him to know this could be a future base of strong solidarity. I was imagining a relationship between the South Bronx and Cuba that could broaden cultural, educational, health, and particularly business encounters, which could prove very beneficial for both if the U.S. trade blockade against Cuba was eliminated. I was thinking in terms of the future of my neighborhood. That is why I was adamant about having a perfect event with the right messages. I wanted President Fidel Castro and the Cuban people to remember the South Bronx as they had remembered Harlem in 1960.

# THINGS GOING WELL, THEN…

By mid-afternoon I was feeling good. Things had gone much smoother than I anticipated. I made all my calls. I first called Carlos Nazario, the president of the National Puerto Rican Business Council, our host organization. I wanted to know if there were any last-minute developments. Carlos ran the Council like he ran his business, really tight, and I was grateful for his support and trust in this venture. Any other person with less courage would have probably backed out when this went from being just a news release to an actual dinner with Fidel Castro. I also thought that since his beverage wholesale distribution business, Metro Beer & Soda, had several Cuban colleagues in the same line of work, some of these Cubans who were not so open-minded about Cuba might have tried to pressure Carlos to back out. I knew at least two of his colleagues were down and out anti-the Cuban revolution and very anti-Fidel, something they let me know on more than one occasion, whenever we had a business encounter. One in particular had almost jumped out of his pants one day when I went to his warehouse to pick up a donation of water for an event that a friend had arranged, wearing a Che Guevara T-shirt. I'll never forget his reaction. He got all wired up and started a harangue about some so-called atrocities that he linked to Che. I tried to be courteous since I was there to pick up the water products for my friend and did not want to be told to leave. I thought some of these business associates might pressure Carlos.

I went back to the office to check on last-minute details. We had no calls, no threats, no reporters, and no one calling to get on the guest list. Most importantly, there were no calls from the U.S. or Cuban secret services and that made me sigh with relief. Each previous call I had received, mainly from the U.S. Secret Service, would churn my stomach, because it was always about a problem or concern. They had also called to brief me on the security measures being utilized for the dinner, warning me that under no circumstances would they allow any of the security procedures to be changed by anyone.

I was able to finally finish my notes on the logistics and began to read Franklin's translation. I remained in the office after everyone had left so that I could rewrite the speech in Spanish. Though my first language was Spanish, growing up on the streets of New York had gradually peeled away much of my native tongue and replaced it with the dominant languages of the streets, English and *mucho* Spanglish. Thus I could read and speak Spanish, but I did feel much more comfortable reading and speaking English.

I decided to stay and retype the Spanish translation, as I believed this would help me remember what I wrote in English. While typing, I noticed that Franklin did more than translate. He also added a few lines here and there. I smiled, as I knew Franklin might do that since he had a better command of Spanish and might express my thoughts more precisely. I agreed with his additions and felt that I had accomplished our goal of writing down the points we wanted to get across.

After typing, I printed a copy, read it a few times and decided it was time to head home. It must have been close to 7 or 8 p.m. I also wanted to go home and read the speech to my wife, Liz who had always been my editor, even when we were in college when she edited many of my term papers. She had a good analytical mind and I respected her opinion. But I had to be home no later than 9 p.m. to catch Liz before she went to sleep, as she was an early bird getting up every morning by 6 a.m. I planned to read the speech a few more times at home, read it to Liz, take a nice warm shower, make some warm relaxing tea, and watch my favorite pre-bedtime program, *Nightline,* which aired on WABC-TV right after the 11 PM news. I knew that doing all that would put me in the perfect mood to forget everything I was doing for the Fidel Castro dinner and put my mind at ease to get a good night's sleep and be ready for D-Day the next day. Boy was I wrong again....

# JIMMY CALLS ME: HE'S NOT A HAPPY CAMPER

Almost as soon as I got home, I got a call from Jimmy Rodríguez. I had not been in touch with him since before we knew Fidel had said yes; instead it was Congressman Serrano who had been in communication with Jimmy. I didn't know what Serrano might have told him about the number of guests. But Jimmy and I never discussed the details of the restaurant other than the use of the banquet facilities in the lower level of the restaurant. We thought that the entire lower level might have to be made private and off-limits to the general public until our event was over. There were some bathrooms and one, or two other smaller rooms that we wanted to make off- limits to the general public as well.

Jimmy and I never discussed logistics when I first called to ask him to allow us to use the restaurant's name in our news release. However, he agreed to hold the event at his restaurant once we knew Fidel had said yes to our invitation.

During my communications with the Secret Service they never asked for any information about the restaurant except to know its location and the name of the owner. They never explained that they had to secure the restaurant the day before the event, and that once it was secured, no one could have access to the restaurant until the event ended the next day. I learned about this when Jimmy called me to tell me the Secret Service had come to his restaurant and asked him to clear it of all patrons and staff so that they could conduct a security check. They brought in dogs and other equipment to secure the restaurant and once they had done so, he was told that the restaurant was "off limits" to everyone, no exceptions.

Understandably, Jimmy was quite upset. He said I had never told him the restaurant was going to have to be closed the night before the event. He said he was going to have a major loss of income, more than he had anticipated. He was already giving us a discount on the price of the dinner; originally estimated to be for 50 people, but what was now closer to more than 300 guests. Now he said, he was also losing even more business; the late night crowd the night before the event as well as the morning breakfast, lunch and early evening dinner crowd on the day of the event. I was silent as Jimmy let out his frustration. I was also shocked, as I did not know that the Secret Service would go to the restaurant and close it a day early. That had never been mentioned. Perhaps that was another one of the Secret Service subtle actions to make the event as difficult as possible so that I would be forced to cancel it. All I could do was apologize to Jimmy. I told him that I had no idea that the Secret Service would do that and that had never been explained to me. I told him that if they had told me that I would have definitely told him and somehow helped him prepare for it.

I was thinking of how much money Jimmy might be losing and how we might be able to make it up to him. I told Jimmy that I would speak to Carlos and other members of the National Puerto Rican Business Council and ask them all to use his restaurant for any and all future personal, or business events. I told him that I would also tell Congressman Serrano to do the same. I told him that I thought that although he was going to lose some business over the next day, he would make that up and more.

I explained that the publicity being generated by the dinner event and the media that had been calling to gain entry to the dinner meant that Jimmy's Bronx Café was becoming known and was getting hundreds of thousands of dollars in free publicity. Jimmy was an astute businessman and knew that what I was telling him was correct. The restaurant had already been receiving some publicity when we sent out the news release and then afterward, once the word was out that Fidel would be coming to the Bronx. Now that it was a confirmed event with Fidel Castro at his restaurant, the publicity was going to go through the roof. I explained that not only would the restaurant be mentioned in local news coverage, Fidel's visit would guarantee, citywide, statewide, nationwide, and even worldwide attention. Jimmy was also a master of publicity and he knew that what I was saying had merit. He relaxed and we agreed to see each other the next day prior to the dinner event. I told him we were going to get there a few hours earlier to help with the setup and logistics.

After putting out this last fire, the rest of the evening was quite calm. I went over the Spanish translation of the speech that I was going to deliver when I was to introduce Congressman Serrano. I did not know what to expect the next day. I thought of something I had learned in the martial arts, "expect the unexpected." I was going to rest this last evening and prepare myself to expect the unexpected the following day.

# MORNING OF - REVIEWING SECURITY

Finally the BIG day was here. I woke up and, remarkably, I felt rested from a good night's sleep. It was as if my mind was also relieved that the past three days of incredible activity were about to come to an end soon.

I decided to go to the office early to check and review all the details one more time. When I got to the office there were no calls from the U.S. or Cuban Secret Service and that was a relief. They had already briefed me on the security measures being utilized for the dinner. So I spent most of the morning making calls to be certain everything was going as anticipated, I was reminding everyone of the serious security measures that would be in place. I also wanted to make sure that we all were still on the same page, no surprises, no changes, especially on the guest list. There could be no additions to the list that had already been submitted to the Secret Service.

I expected the entrance and area near the restaurant to be chaotic and filled with local uniformed and undercover police, and with demonstrators, both for and against Fidel's visit. Jimmy's Bronx Cafe took up an entire city block. The structure was built from scratch with Jimmy supervising every step; it was Jimmy's dream. He had put a lot of his personal touch into the planning and later construction of this huge building. He wanted to build more than a restaurant; he wanted to also fill the void that existed in the Bronx, especially in the South Bronx, of quality banquet, dining and dance club facilities. Jimmy's dream was to have it all under one roof. That's why Jimmy's Bronx Café took up that entire block and that is why it became an instant success. Jimmy's provided a venue of pride for the Puerto Rican, Latino and African-American communities of the South Bronx that no one else had done.

It was the last building on the extreme west side of Fordham Road, at the foot of the Fordham Avenue Bridge to Manhattan with both the south and north entrances to the Deegan Expressway on the northern and southern side of Fordham Road. The restaurant overlooked the Deegan Expressway and the Harlem River on the west. Fordham Road, one of the busiest streets in the Bronx, was on its south side. On the north side, an abandoned lot with a lot of trees and shrubs bordered the restaurant that also served as a possible parking lot for those that did not mind walking over dirt and rocks. The easiest walking path was from the east side of Fordham Road. That block had a huge indoor storage/parking facility, and the Secret Service wanted all guests to enter from that corner.

I was sure that the restaurant's location with its busy and varied landscape was one of the reasons that the Secret Service did not want to have this event in the Bronx. It was going to require a lot of resources to secure a perimeter around the restaurant, something totally different from the Manhattan office buildings where they had been providing security for Fidel. I wanted to make sure that our guests avoided all of that anticipated commotion by making sure that they knew where and how to correctly enter the restaurant.

The Secret Service had explained that several hours prior to Fidel's arrival, they would set up three levels of security around the restaurant, or in their words, three "perimeters." One was one block away from the restaurant, the second was across the street, and third was at the entrance to and inside the restaurant.

All access, as well as pedestrian traffic, was going to be cut off from a block away. Everyone entering the restaurant had to have his or her names on the guest list that had already been submitted to the Secret Service. They were required to have a government-issued identification to verify their identity and prove they were the person on the list. They made it perfectly clear that if a person's name was not on the list, or if the person did not have proper identification, that person would not be allowed to enter.

Once the person went through the first perimeter they then had to walk down the block across the street from the restaurant. In order to proceed through that second checkpoint, they again had to be checked against the list provided. If they were cleared on that second list, they then were allowed to cross the street to the entrance of the restaurant where they then had to be checked for a third time against the same list. Once they cleared that list, they walked through a metal detector, had their bags and purses checked, and then walked to a table where our people checked them off against our copy of the guest list. We then would give them a nametag and colored round tag, which they had to visibly place on their chest, collar, or lapel. The Secret Service security instructed us to use two colors for the dots on all the name tags; blue for guests who had access to the banquet hall only, and red for those of us working on the organizing committee with access to all areas of the restaurant, except those areas placed off limits by the Secret Service.

When I called Carlos and Congressman Serrano I stressed the security measures, because I knew that access to the dinner location was out of our control. If a guest could not go through the security measures that the Secret Service had set up, none of us would be able to do anything about it.

# READY FOR WHATEVER &
# FEELING GOOD ABOUT IT

I kept on thinking, this was it; today was "D-Day." I had worked on many campaigns and projects as an activist and volunteered for many causes, but I had never worked so hard with so little time for something that was so important and meaningful. Putting together an event that was not on anyone's radar with a world-renowned figure like Fidel Castro, and to make that happen in less than 72 hours, was close to a miracle. I was very proud of what it appeared we had accomplished. To know that on this evening Fidel Castro, one of the most respected and controversial figures alive was going to come to a dinner that I had directly helped to make happen was overwhelming. I could not help thinking of my father's quote, "*Todo es posible,*" (everything is possible). I felt good knowing how well we handled the surprise that we would actually be putting on a dinner for President Fidel Castro that none of us dreamed would occur. However, after learning of Fidel's acceptance we ran with it and accomplished what most thought impossible. We overcame all the obstacles, problems and concerns and the event was on as scheduled.

The morning went by so quickly I could hardly believe it. It was now close to 1 p.m., so, I decided to close the office, have lunch and head for home to get ready to leave around 3 p.m. for the restaurant.

Mickey called to ask if I was driving to the restaurant. I told him I was because I had a few things to take to help set up. We agreed he would meet me at my apartment on the Grand Concourse and we would drive over together.

I began to get ready by 2 p.m. It was a strange feeling in that I was very selective about everything, including on what to wear. It was like one of those special events, like a wedding, or a first-time job interview, when you want to make sure that you make a good impression. Except that in this case, I was unsure as to whom it was it that I wanted to impress. I just knew that this was one of the most important events that I had participated in and I wanted to look my best. I decided on a dark, business suit, white shirt and a red tie. I don't remember if I chose the tie as a symbol of power, which is what a red tie usually represents, or because I knew red was also the color of revolution and that it would go quite well with the event. I learned a lot about how to dress, from a very close brother, Felipe Luciano, who in my opinion was a debonair dresser. Felipe had gone from being a radical-dressing Young Lord and member of the Last Poets, a cultural group active in the late 1960s, to being a pioneer in corporate media in New York prime time television. Felipe knew how to make an impression and dress for success. I was always grateful how he took a rookie like me under his wing when I got my first most important job in City Hall and taught me what to expect from a high profile position in city government. I was glad to have learned from one of the best and this night I would apply everything I learned from him.

* * *

# DRIVE TO DINNER: AN
# UNEXPECTED PRESENT

Mickey arrived at my place at 3 p.m., as usual on time. As we drove to the restaurant, Mickey handed me a gift, the book *History will Absolve Me*, based on Fidel's epic summation at his trial when he served as his own defense council for the July 26, 1953 attack on the Moncada Garrison in Cuba — the July 26, 1953 assault that kicked off the Cuban Revolution. Mickey told me that I should try and get Fidel to autograph the book. I was surprised, as I was not expecting any gift. I thought that it was a thoughtful and considerate gesture. I thanked him and we talked about the book and the significance of getting an autograph from Fidel Castro. I was so involved in the here and now of planning for the dinner that I was not seeing what perhaps Mickey was already seeing as the historic event in which we were about to participate in.

It was a great idea to see about having Fidel sign the book. I was too involved in the event and all of its ramifications to think of having anything signed, or keeping any memorabilia from it. I was glad and grateful that I had someone like Mickey who was able to see the value of having something personal from that historic event.

I cherished that book and what Fidel wrote to me that was not only quite personal but also captured everything about that crazy idea that turned into history in the making. I kept that book on my library in our apartment on a shelf with several other books on Latin America. I would only show it off to a few selected people who visited my apartment. Years later I went to look for it, and it was gone. To this day I feel really bad about losing that book. I have a few items that I have collected throughout the years that have a lot of personal value because of whom they are from, or whom they are about. I have the entire collection of Roberto Clemente baseball cards. I also have a painting from a very good no-name painter who made it big before passing. His name was Guichy and he was from my hometown, Guayama, Puerto Rico. I remember seeing Guichy painting in his garage during a visit to Guayama when I was in college. I fell in love with the painting because it depicted a beautiful flamboyan tree by the Guamani River, a place I remembered from my childhood. I wound up buying that painting in installments and Guichi went on to become a well-known and respected painter who exhibited in Puerto Rico and in Europe. That painting has a lot of value for me, but that personalized book from President Fidel Castro would have been my #1 collectible item today.

# SETTING UP AND WAITING FOR FIDEL

After setting up most of the banners and tables and reviewing the security procedures with our own security team, we waited for the people to arrive. These included employees, volunteers, members of the Cuban Mission and guests who were beginning to arrive earlier than expected. We guessed those people did not want to miss the opportunity to be present at what was already considered the #1 Latino event in the city.

Banners, sound system, podium all of the set up being done
prior to Fidel's visit. (Photo Personal Archives)

Soon many more guests began to arrive, and the situation inside Jimmy's Bronx Cafe became one of organized chaos. Security did their job in making sure that only the people that were on the list were allowed to enter the first two perimeters of security leading to the restaurant. Once they got to the main entrance they had to go through another level of security; they were searched and had to pass through a metal detector that had been set up at the main entrance of the restaurant. Then they were given a nametag and told where they would be sitting.

This last level of security was creating a problem, as the line to get in was moving very slowly. The problem was that everyone had to go through a metal detector with secret service agents on both sides. Guests with bags, or women with purses had to open them and have them inspected before they went through the metal detector. But even after they passed through the detector, they had to stop at our table and be checked against the master list that we had given the Secret Service prior to the event. The Secret Service would not let anyone go past the table until they were checked, and given a nametag and knew where they were going to sit.

This final step was creating a serious backlog. I noticed that there was a major confusion between the Secret Service agent and the person manning the table. We thought that once a guest went through the main entrance and passed through the various security checkpoints, the last thing they would have to do would be to go to the main table to get their name tag and seat assignment. The Secret Service never told me that we had to have someone from our work group at the door to work in unison with his or her agents as the last step once entering the restaurant prior to proceeding to the banquet hall.

Since we did not plan for that we thought that one of Jimmy's restaurant staffers could handle that small detail. Unfortunately, it was not working out and people were bottlenecking between the metal detectors and the table we had set up inside the restaurant. We wanted people to be able to move along quickly and easily to flow into the restaurant and down to the banquet hall and be seated as soon as they came in because we were not sure how they would be bringing Fidel into the restaurant and we wanted to keep the main entrance clear.

I realized the problem was with our check-in table. The restaurant employee who had been assigned to the table was not familiar with our guest list and spoke limited English. We needed someone at the table who was bilingual, who knew many of the guests, and was familiar with the restaurant and our procedures. We had no one available since everyone from our planning committee had a specific assignment. Franklin and Mickey were already handling more than we had anticipated, helping to seat people and putting out small fires with guests who had issues as to where they were sitting, who was at the table with them, or handling special VIP guest, or guests from the Cuban Mission. Kimberly was my liaison with all the waiters and restaurant staff that were working the banquet to make sure that everything was going smoothly. We did not want people being served dinner when President Fidel Castro arrived or during any of the presentations. I also did not want to ask Jerry Fontanez to pull any of the embedded security people he had to man a table. The closest person I could think of, who was walking with me at the time, was my son, Julio Antonio.

Julio Antonio had visited the restaurant many times and had seen it even when it was under construction, so he knew the physical layout. Jimmy had a close relationship with my children and treated them like family. In fact, his former restaurant, Mariscos Del Caribe on Webster Avenue and the Cross Bronx Expressway, and the new Jimmy's Bronx Cafe restaurants had at times been impromptu childcare centers for me. Julio felt comfortable in the restaurant, he knew almost all of the staff, and he also knew many of the guests, since he had been working with me in the streets of the South Bronx from the time he was a five-year-old boy. In fact, he was the youngest campaign volunteer that José Serrano had in his historic campaign for Bronx borough president in 1985.[xi] Thus, 15- year-old Julito (Spanish for little Julio, as close family and friends called him) became the gatekeeper who worked directly with the Secret Service on processing all the guests on their final step to enter the dinner. I briefed him and watched as he processed a few of the many guests that were congregating at the entrance. The Secret Service was working well with him and he with them. Now I could leave and race outside where I was told that another situation was brewing.

## NEIGHBORHOOD WAITS IN AWE;
## PROTESTORS FOR HIRE

Outside the restaurant things were jumping. The neighborhood surrounding the restaurant was intrigued by everything that was going on. Having many police cars in the neighborhood is not a rare thing in the South Bronx; however, having traffic diverted, and not allowed to park, or stop anywhere near the restaurant, and having police sharpshooters on every roof facing the restaurant, was another thing. This went along with not allowing people on their roofs or fire escapes, having a helicopter circling every couple of minutes, a police gunboat on the river, and having the community swarmed by undercover personnel and vehicles. This was something that none of the residents and storefront business owners had ever seen, or experienced.

If that was not enough, there were two groups of vocal protesters. Each across the street from each other separated by wooden police barricades, and police officers. This was not surprising, because according to New York City Police records, 58 demonstrations were organized to take place in New York City during the few days of the United Nations' 50th anniversary. More than half of the rallies and demonstration planned involved Cuba.

I walked over to the south corner of the restaurant to see where all the commotion and noise was coming from and saw the two groups. I acknowledged the group supporting Fidel's visit. I knew that many of them were people who had called asking for a ticket to attend the dinner, but unfortunately we could not oblige. I wanted to thank them for understanding and reiterated that the restaurant was full to capacity. They appreciated that I walked over to speak to them. They were there to show support for President Fidel Castro and his visit to the Bronx and perhaps get a glimpse of him when his motorcade came by. Others were there simply to show support for an event that demonstrated to Mayor Giuliani that by disinviting Castro he had disrespected a Latino guest and the Puerto Rican/Latino community. Still others were there demonstrating their support for the invitation to Castro to come to the heart of the Puerto Rican community, the Bronx.

As I was crossing the street to return to the restaurant I looked over to the group that was protesting his visit. It was not the "large" group that I was told inside. From a glance, I could see perhaps fifty people. But to my great surprise, I recognized a few of them. These were guys that I knew from the streets where I had grown up, Cauldwell, Trinity, and St. Ann's Avenue; marginalized guys who were always looking for a way to make a dollar to survive. They were not into politics, or any particular way of thinking other than surviving. I had helped them on many occasions to find part-time work, or writing a letter of support to get them, or a family member into a drug rehab program, special housing, or for a parole officer. I never judged, or ignored them, and as such I also received a lot of respect and support from them when I walked through the streets of the South Bronx.

When I walked up to them they were surprised and happy to see me. I was surprised, but not happy, to see them protesting our dinner. We greeted each other and I communicated with my hand, face and arm motion, "What the fuck are you doing here?" I knew they had no political take on the dinner or Fidel, so as such I was interested in knowing why they were there holding up cardboard signs with anti-Fidel, anti-Cuba slogans. They immediately realized that they were protesting against something that I was supporting; therefore they were protesting against me. At that moment a few of the other protesters came over to yell at me, but as these guys had done many times in the past they protected me and in their more natural state turned around and told them to "back the fuck up." That was the end of that potential confrontation. It was obvious that many of those that were protesting were not from the community and probably not from the city.

As we continued to talk, a few police officers walked over to me, but I told them everything was fine and they walked back to their post. My young friends explained that they did not know what this was about, but that they were being paid $50 each to be there and protest. When they told me that, I immediately changed my tone and told them that I understood. When I asked who was paying them, they all answered, Reverend Ruben Díaz. As was my habit, I turned the situation into a "Teachable Moment" and quickly explained to them what was taking place and why we were having the dinner. Like most street savvy people, when given respect and information, they immediately understood what was happening. One of them suggested that they drop the signs and join the pro-Fidel demonstrators across the street. I discouraged them from doing that and losing the opportunity to make their money. I knew how difficult it was for these guys to make an honest dollar and $50 dollars to just stand there with a sign was easier than something else they could have been doing in the streets that also could have gotten them into some type of trouble. They laughed and told me, "*Ya nos pagaron,*" (we already got paid). I laughed as well. We agreed that they would stay for a few more minutes and leave.

I later learned that Reverend Ruben Díaz was not the one that paid them, but was instead simply the conduit for them to get paid by the Cuban American National Foundation, widely-known in the 1990s as a well - funded anti-Cuba, anti-Fidel Castro organization that had raised millions of dollars through private and government sources not only to lobby, but also allegedly to work to sabotage any act of friendship toward or support for Cuba. Jorge

Mas Canosa headed the organization. I also learned that the Foundation contacted Bronx State Senator, Efrain González to help recruit protestors, but Senator González refused to help because he did not want to do anything against Jimmy's Bronx Café because of his friendship with Jimmy.[xii]

The foundation had a lot of money to spread around New York City to back its efforts to embarrass President Castro and show mass support for their call to tighten sanctions against Cuba. The foundation was allegedly spending its money in New York to create an environment to undermine Fidel Castro's visit to liberal New York, progressive Harlem, and revolutionary South Bronx.

* ✳ ✳

## THE PRESS WANTED IN - THE
## BOROUGH PRESIDENT WANTS OUT

As I walked back another situation was developing with the media at the front entrance. The number of journalists on the scene had grown. Apparently they had all been cleared by the Secret Service and as such thought that gave them access to enter the restaurant and cover the dinner. Every major news station and network was present. We also had many smaller independent local cable networks and local weekly papers. I had people showing me their credentials, insisting that they were told that they could cover the event.

At no time had we thought of assigning anyone to handle the media because we did not see this as a press event. This whole thing began with a simple news release inviting Fidel to come to the Bronx in response to Mayor Giuliani's act of snubbing him from a city-planned dinner. For us, the likelihood that Fidel Castro would actually say yes to our invitation was like the odds of winning the lottery. We only found out on Saturday when he arrived that President Castro had accepted our invitation to come to a dinner on Monday, a day that none of us expected to be worked into Fidel's busy schedule. This did not give us much time to do anything but plan the event. We never thought of a press event, thus we never considered a major press presence.

The fact was that after learning that Fidel had accepted our invitation; we did everything possible to avoid the press. We believed the less publicity we received the fewer problems we would have. That is why we never put out a follow-up news release to say that Fidel had accepted our invitation and was coming to the Bronx. Once we learned that Fidel was actually coming, we did not want much publicity because we felt that would focus more attention on us and prompt everyone from supporters of the visit to those against it to contact us, which would sidetrack us from the work we knew we needed to do to make this dinner a success.

We knew once people learned that President Castro was coming to the Bronx and specifically to Jimmy's Bronx Café, we would not be able to control the requests from people wanting tickets, calling the restaurant for reservations, or possibly harassing members of the National Puerto Rican Business Council, or Congressman Serrano's office to name just a few of our concerns. So I purposely tried to keep the media off our heels as much as possible.

Unfortunately, the information about Fidel's acceptance of our invitation still seemed to be trickling down from those who were getting information about Fidel's itinerary from the Secret Service or by calling Congressman Serrano's office where aides confirmed that Fidel was coming to the Bronx. Once the news was out that Fidel was coming, the press went on a free-for-all, interviewing whomever they could. We received many requests and I instructed Kimberly to refer all journalists to either Congressman Serrano's office or to the president of the National Puerto Rican Business Council, Carlos Nazario. However, the media also went to the restaurant to speak with Jimmy and even interviewed Jimmy's Executive Chef, Joe Torres. When they asked Joe, how he felt about "feeding Fidel Castro," Joe replied that he was a chef and was there "to feed whomever came in through that door."

They also interviewed people who lived in the neighborhood and owners or managers of small businesses near the restaurant. For the most part it seemed the press was looking for major controversy from the community, something that they did not did get. Apparently the media did not understand what many of us who walk and work in the streets knew, that the majority of the people that heard the details of the dinner and Fidel's visit had no problem with Fidel coming to the Bronx. In fact, many expressed respect for Fidel for coming to a neighborhood that few citywide, statewide, or nationally elected officials ever visited (except for President Jimmy Carter who visited Charlotte Street in 1977).

The general feeling on the streets in the days before the dinner was one of support. The South Bronx is one of the poorest congressional districts in the country and very rarely received any positive attention. Now because of Fidel Castro's visit, the South Bronx was in the national and even international spotlight. It was as if everyone living in the South Bronx was getting his or her fifteen minutes of fame. This was something that even the poorest, most marginalized, and least educated people in our borough knew and they respected Fidel for it. Fidel's visit to Harlem in his previous visit to New York City in 1960 was well documented and won the respect of the African-American community. Now he was visiting the South Bronx and the Puerto Rican/Latino community felt the same way.

Unfortunately, not everyone in our borough felt that sense of pride and respect for Fidel's visit. Our own Puerto Rican Bronx Borough President, Fernando Ferrer, was against the visit. I don't know if that was because he was probably not invited by Congressman Serrano who was the main person inviting the elected officials and many of the VIP guests. Or if, as it was rumored, perhaps some promises of future contributions from right-wing Cubans had also persuaded the borough president to disinvite Fidel as well. However, since this dinner was not organized or sponsored by the borough president, all he could do was send out a news release. "If Castro wants to visit the Bronx, that's his business," Ferrer said in a statement. "For my part and as borough president, I cannot in good conscience extend a welcome to any person who has been charged with violating human rights." Many of us saw this as yet another action by a borough president who was totally out of step with the true feelings of his constituents.

# CONDUCTING MY OWN FOCUS GROUP IN THE STREETS

Throughout this entire whirlwind of events I never thought or dreamed that I would meet Fidel Castro. As strange as it might sound, though this whole event was centered on President Castro, I was never thinking about spending any time with him. My mind was consumed with the overwhelming details that were unexpectedly thrown on my plate — organizing a dinner banquet for over 300 guests in two days and dealing with security for the event. However, my major concern was with security inside and outside of the restaurant. The Secret Service had not wanted the event to take place in the Bronx; I felt under pressure to make sure that nothing happened at the event. I kept thinking if there had been so many attempts to assassinate President Castro, could there be another attempt while he was here? If anything happened to him in the South Bronx, I would probably be remembered as the guy who was responsible. I had never been interested in leaving any legacy to my name other than being a good provider for my children. However, I was definitely not willing to allow my name to become synonymous with something happening to Fidel Castro in an activity that I had coordinated. There was no way I would live with that.

So security, beyond that provided by both the American and Cuban government agencies, was on my mind a lot. The presence of the two official security teams was not enough to calm my apprehension. Providing our own private and secret security inside the restaurant with Jerry and his crew made me feel a lot better, but I still had concerns.

The South Bronx was our home turf and I felt we had to be ready for the unexpected and that is where I focused my attention. I had spent many hours before the event checking out areas of the restaurant that I already knew quite well, but I wanted to make sure there were no changes. I also walked the streets, particularly the perimeter of the restaurant. I knew several of the community folks who tend to spend a lot of time in the streets and who knew everything that went on in the hood. I had told them of the pending visit and told them that they were going to see a lot of activity, police, and undercover agents, before and during the visit of President Fidel Castro. Some were surprised and others skeptical to hear that Fidel Castro was coming to their neighborhood. They all knew, or had heard of well - known and popular musicians, actors and baseball stars visiting Jimmy's Bronx Cafe, but the visit of President Fidel Castro of Cuba was something totally different; this was at another level.

They were all excited to hear the news. They seemed to admire President Castro, who had led his country in a revolution that had survived the wrath of the United States, the most powerful country in the world. Most of the neighbors were from Puerto Rico or the Dominican Republic and both islands had a very close relationship to Cuba. Many knew the history of all three islands and their struggle to liberate themselves from the Spanish colonization that had dominated the islands for almost four centuries.

Some even knew of the existence of the *Confederación Antillana* (Antillean Confederation). The Antillean Confederation was an idea that flourished in the mid-1800s that was promulgated by Puerto Rican liberators, Dr. Ramón Emeterio Betances, Eugenio María De Hostos, José De Diego; the Cuban national hero José Martí; and Gregorio Luperón of the Dominican Republic. They argued that the islands of the Spanish Greater Antilles needed to join together to become a regional authority to seek the sovereignty and welfare of Cuba, the Dominican Republic and Puerto Rico, and bring the three islands together as one country.

The idea was to end European colonialism in America, as well as to respond to the U.S. Monroe Doctrine and its phrase of "America for Americans," with the change in terminology suggested by Betances: "Greater Antilles for Antillanos." The Caribbean idealists met in the port of San Felipe in Puerto Plata in the Dominican Republic where they agreed on a new flag and a constitution for the country they hoped would come into being. The flag would be the one that the Puerto Rican revolutionaries flew in the Grito de Lares revolt of 1868, which was copied from the Dominican flag except that the colors were inverted.

The plan was foiled when the U.S. battleship *USS Maine* mysteriously exploded in the port of La Habana in 1898; hundreds of US sailors were killed. The U.S. accused Spain of blowing up the ship, and started the Spanish American War that lasted just a few weeks. When the war ended, so did Spanish rule in the Caribbean. The islands came under U.S. control, effectively killing the idea of creating *La Confederación Antillana*.

But somehow the ties between Cuba, the Dominican Republic and Puerto Rico had trickled down to the present and into the streets of the neighborhood around Jimmy's restaurant because there was no one—and I mean no one—who I spoke with who had anything negative to say about Fidel's visit. This made me feel that the surrounding community had our back and would be our surveillance in the streets surrounding the restaurant and that made me feel very comfortable.

## OUTSIDE THE RESTAURANT AND
## GETTING CLOSER TO FIDEL'S VISIT

The issue now confronting me was that every journalist gathering outside the restaurant—and there were at least 50 of them —wanted to get in to cover the event. I told them that there was no way that we were going to allow everyone access, reminding them that this was a private dinner and that we were full to capacity. However, I also knew that this was turning into a historic event that should be documented. So I offered them a deal. I would allow a few major networks inside if they agreed to our rules. They would be escorted to an area that would be cordoned off, where they would be able to film, take pictures, and record. If for any reason they walked out of that area they would be escorted out, no exceptions. I also reminded them that this was not a press event, but a private dinner, so they would not be allowed to ask questions or to try to interview anyone. They could interview any members of the organizing committee, or any guest after Fidel left. Finally, I explained that since we could not allow every TV network access to film, we would allow any major station in that would provide a feeder to the others outside who we could not accommodate. I believe CNN volunteered to provide a feeder. I also remember giving access to the Hispanic Information and Telecommunications Network (HITN), a Latino non-commercial news organization recommended by Assemblyman José Rivera, with the understanding that they would provide us with a copy of everything they filmed (we never received anything from them).

That settled the issue of the press, and finally I returned back inside the restaurant to see how things were going. Someone from the Cuban mission told me Fidel was on his way. I could not wait; I wanted this event to start because it seemed every minute there was something else that needed my attention.

I was anxious for President Castro's motorcade to arrive. I spent most of my time going from the downstairs banquet hall to the upstairs entrance, looking out the front windows to see how the demonstrations were doing, and checking in with our core group. I inspected every inch of the restaurant that we were allowed to walk through. I wanted to make sure that everything was as planned. We had walkie-talkies to communicate among ourselves. I spent time checking in and making my rounds. I would constantly check in with Jerry and our own internal security team. I also spoke periodically with Bruno Rodríguez, the Cuban Minister at the United Nations with who I had been in constant contact since Fidel confirmed his attendance. He was the Cuban point person at the restaurant working with us to ensure that everything was under control while we waited for Fidel to arrive.

We knew that President Castro was on his way and Jimmy, or one of his staff would communicate with me every so often to see if I had any idea when Fidel would arrive so they could be to sure that the food was ready to serve. My answer was always the same; that I would let them know as soon as I knew. When we learned that President Castro was coming from another engagement where they were going to eat prior to attending our event, we decided to begin serving everyone. The idea was for everyone to be served before Fidel arrived so that we would not waste time, or interrupt with the noise of people eating, plates being moved and waiters walking around. Once President Castro entered the building we wanted as little commotion as possible.

* * *

# HAVANA - WE HAVE A PROBLEM

The restaurant's banquet hall was filling up to capacity and the majority of the guests were already inside and waiting for the big moment. There was a lot of positive energy in the restaurant; everyone was smiling and making toasts, and there was a lot of networking taking place. Everyone seemed happy to be present. It was interesting to me, because I remember several of them telling me when they were first invited that they had no love for Castro or the Cuban revolution, but would attend out of respect and to show their dissatisfaction with the mayor's decision to disinvite President Fidel Castro from his city-sponsored dinner. Others had made snide remarks when asked for additional information that was required for them to be cleared by security. But now the atmosphere felt festive, like waiting for a popular star to arrive.

I continued my rounds. When I went upstairs to the main entrance I was told that Bruno Rodríguez, the Cuban Mission head, was looking for me. The banquet hall was jumping with people everywhere, and it took a few minutes before Bruno and I found each other. Bruno had a serious look on his face, took me to a corner and told me that we had a problem!

As customary in these circumstances, I always imagined the worst and then worked my way down to a less serious problem. So with the expression on Bruno

Rodríguez's face and the urgency of his approach, I was preparing myself for him to tell me that Fidel was not coming, that something important came up and he had to cancel. Or perhaps the Secret Service had found a reason to cancel, or something like that. However, Bruno mentioned none of that. He said there was a woman present who had entered as a member of the press; she had been identified as an instigator at a number of past activities with the Cuban government. He told me that they would recommend that Fidel stay away if this woman was not compelled to leave. "What a relief," I thought. "That's easy!" I would just get the Secret Service to escort this woman out. I asked Bruno for her name and assured him that I would take care of the problem.

Unfortunately that was easier said than done. Bruno gave me her name and I immediately concentrated on putting out this newest fire. Via my walkie-talkie, I asked my team if anyone could locate the head of the U.S. Secret Service. In a few minutes I was given his location. I went to find him and tell him of our situation and ask for his assistance.

I told him what Bruno Rodríguez had told me, that there was someone present who had falsely entered as a member of the media; but since she was not a journalist and was not on our guest list, and considered an agitator by the Cubans she was not welcomed. I said I wanted her to be escorted out of the restaurant. To my surprise, the security liaison told me that he could not do anything about that situation. He said their job was not to escort people out, and that if the person was not a direct physical threat, or danger to President Castro and if she had proper press credentials that they did not have any reason to intervene. I was shocked at his response and could not believe that the Secret Service, which was responsible for Fidel Castro's safety, was not going to do anything about this woman who was obviously a concern to the officials from the Cuban Mission.

I remember raising my voice, getting a bit agitated, and asking, "How can this not be your concern?" I reiterated with emphasis that the head of the Cuban Mission in the United Nations had a concern to the point that President Castro might not attend. Again, I questioned how could this not be of interest to him and the U.S. Secret Service? I wanted to make sure that I heard him correctly. I again raised my concern, pausing after every word. I remember telling him: *There was - a - person - in - the – building – that - the - Cuban - government - had - informed - us - that - she - was - a – threat. That - she -had -been –involved - in - a - number -of - disruptive - events - against - the - Cuban - government - in - the - past, - how - could - this - not - be - a - concern - for you as well?*

I asked why the fact that this person might cause a major disruption while Fidel was present would that not be his concern? He said I had just told him that Fidel would not come if she were present; therefore, it was not going to be a problem.

With that response I finally got the hint as to why he was not about to do anything. It was not that he was careless and did not care about Fidel's security. It was that the best security for Fidel in his opinion was for him not to come to the South Bronx. I remembered how they had tried to convince me to cancel the dinner and then when I refused to do that, tried to get me to move the event to Manhattan, because they thought it was better for the dinner to be held there and not in the South Bronx. Obviously, he was not going to help us with this issue. He probably would have loved for Fidel to cancel coming to the Bronx. Well, fortunately for us I was ready to go with PLAN B.

The stage at the main ballroom at Jimmy's Bronx Café would have remained empty if we did not remove the instigator that the Cuban security had identified.

# PLAN B: OUR OWN INTERNAL
# SECURITY TO THE RESCUE

I knew what I had to do. We had to escort this woman out of the building, but it had to be done tactfully. I used my walkie-talkie to call for our
own security. This is not what I expected. We had gone through many hours
of extensive review of the names of everyone invited. Every name had to go
through my office before I submitted them to both the U.S. and the Cuban
secret services. Mickey and Franklin also reviewed many of the names on the
list. According to us, there was no one on that list that one of us did not know
personally, or by association with someone that we could hold accountable.
Unfortunately, the press list did not go through our screening process because
we never planned, or invited them. All of the press that showed up outside
prior to the dinner was screened by the secret service, not by us. Now we had a
situation that I never expected to use our own internal security for. I expected
the Secret Service to handle most security issues inside and, together with
the New York Police Department, all security issues outside the restaurant.
I walked away from the encounter with the Secret Service agent angry and
confused.

I was angry that the Secret Service did not want to deal with the security
issue presented by a person inside the restaurant who had been identified by

the Cubans as a disruptive person who they did not want to be present when Fidel arrived. I was confused about the true nature of the Secret Service, or this particular agent's true intentions regarding the security for Fidel. Was he not supposed to be in charge of security for the event? Supposed this woman was more than a disruptive instigator, should he not want to at least question her motives and intentions? Why would he tell me in so many unsaid words, "This is your problem"?

All of these thoughts were racing through my head as I called out to Jerry, the head of our own internal security, to meet me at the entrance to the banquet hall. Fidel's motorcade was heading towards the Bronx and I wanted to resolve this issue as soon as possible. By the time I got to the bottom floor where the banquet hall was, Jerry was there waiting for me. In his usual short sentences he asked, "What's up?"

I explained what the Cuban Mission head, Bruno Rodríguez, had told me about the unwanted person and what the secret service agent had said. Jerry, a man of few words, said, "We got this!" He went to look for a member of his team and returned with the only female who was part of his security detail – his wife. The three of us then headed to the center of the banquet hall where we had cordoned off a working area for the press.

When we got to the press area there was a lot of activity. Everyone was moving, busy setting up, and making it difficult for us to identify the person. Finally, I noticed the woman that Bruno had described talking to a camera-person. We walked up to her and I introduced myself. I reached out to look at her press credentials and her nametag to verify that indeed she was the person in question. When everything matched with what I was told, I told her that unfortunately, she would have to leave the restaurant. She seemed to be startled and asked me in a loud voice, "*¿Porque?*" (Why?). I told her that our guests from the Cuban Mission had informed me that she was a person with whom they had many negative experiences and therefore she had to leave. She raised her voice a pitch louder and told me in a very indignant manner: "*Esto* *no es Cuba, esto es América, aquí hay democracia. Y no me voy."* (This is not Cuba, this is America, and here there is democracy. I'm not leaving!). I remembered answering, "This is not Cuba, but this is a private dinner and you're not welcome, so you will have to leave." At that moment I turned away from her, gave Jerry the nod and walked away. I did not see exactly what, or how Jerry and his wife (also a black belt) handled the situation. I heard no screaming or noise, just a little scuffle. All I know is that in a matter of minutes the woman and her cameraman were outside the building. Once outside she was no longer our problem, now the secret service, or NYPD had to deal with her. Both, her and her cameraman looked a bit frazzled and upset, but otherwise fine. I found Bruno and told him that the person had been removed. Apparently, he already knew and told me Fidel was minutes away.

# INVITATION TO GREET AND WELCOME
# PRESIDENT FIDEL CASTRO

N ow that the situation with the unwanted guest was over and President Castro was minutes away I was more relaxed. I went over to see how my family were doing and decided to wait there until our guest arrived. We were told by one of the members of the Cuban Mission that Fidel's entourage was getting closer. That made all of us on the organizing committee excited, but also a bit nervous, as we wanted to make sure that everything at the banquet hall was in order. I called out on the walkie-talkie and told all our volunteers that we needed to have everything ready as Fidel's motorcade was approaching. Mickey Melendez and I went by the stage double-checking the microphones and the podium. We made the announcement that our guest of honor was minutes away. You could sense the atmosphere tightening up a bit. The energy was elevated to higher level and everyone began to take their positions and find their assigned seats.

When Mickey and I finished checking all the sound equipment at the podium, Bruno approached and told me that he wanted me to come with him to the loading dock to receive and personally meet Fidel. I was surprised since that was something that I was not expecting. I had been so overwhelmed with all of the planning, coordination, and security for the event that meeting President Fidel Castro never crossed my mind.

I thanked Bruno for the invitation, but told him that perhaps he should invite Congressman Serrano whom as our congressman was the highest - ranking elected official in our group. I believed he was the more appropriate person to meet and receive President Fidel Castro. However, Bruno answered, *"Tu fuiste el que organizaste el evento y queremos que seas tu que lo reciba."* (You were the one that organized the event and we want you to be the one to receive him).

Mickey Melendez was standing close to me and heard our conversation. Mickey looked at me like he was trying to talk to me with his eyes. I could sense that he was saying: *"ARE YOU CRAZY? SAY YES!"* He was not speaking but his body and face said it all. I could also sense that he was telling me, "Take me with you." I then asked Bruno if Mickey could also come with me and he said yes. So I agreed to go meet and receive President Fidel Castro.

Mickey and I looked at each other and followed Bruno like two students following a teacher into a principal's office for a special recognition, or award. It was like we knew that something special was about to happen. Though we were walking straight and tall, inside we were really jumping for joy like happy children about to go to Toys R Us. My heart was pounding and I would guess that Mickey's was pounding as well. My brain as usual was racing, observing the tight security around us.

Bruno took us to the back door leading out of the banquet hall where one of the Secret Service agents was waiting. He took us through several sectors of the restaurant that were off limits and secured and only accessible to the Secret Service. We walked through the serving quarters of the banquet hall, through the long hallway, and pass another swinging metal door with another secret service agent leading into an area near the garage/loading area.

We were held there for a few minutes. My mind began to run off again as my heart continued to pound. This was not like the other times when my mind and heart had raced, reacting to a dangerous circumstances in the South

Bronx, or to an exciting situation. This was different; I was not afraid, but nervous about meeting a person who I had been brainwashed to think was a villain since I was a child. Thanks to my education, I no longer believed those absurd lies, but still my mind was racing and wondering how I, a regular guy from the South Bronx, should greet President Fidel Castro?

Meeting a person who as a law student defied the status quo dictatorship of his country, who then organized and led an armed revolution, who recruited, commanded and then fought alongside legends like Ernesto "Che" Guevara and Camilo Cienfuegos, and who had survived so many assassination attempts, was not like meeting just any celebrity. What would I say? How should I address him? Should I sound official and address him as, Mr. President, or should I address him as a revolutionary leader, as *Comandante*, like many revolutionaries addressed him, or should I address him as the majority of the Cuban people have always addressed him, simply as, Fidel? I was also wondering how would we be introduced? My brain was racing a mile a minute with questions, however it settled when we were finally cleared to enter the garage area.

# U.S. SECURITY DETAIL - ALL THIS FOR FIDEL?

When we entered, Mickey, Bruno, and I stood near the doors where we had just entered with secret service agents positioned at different areas by the doors waiting for the motorcade. We waited not more than two minutes when without notice, the huge metal garage gates in front of us began to be raised slowly. The back of the restaurant faced Landing Place, a street with nothing but an empty lot, across from us, giving us a clear view. As the gates opened we could immediately see a number of New York City police cars leading the motorcade, no sirens, just the lights flashing. We saw four police cars pass. Immediately after the police cars went by, we counted at least three, or four large black SUV's with red lights flashing. Though there were over 180 foreign delegates in New York City for this United Nations fiftieth anniversary gathering and all had to have some type of security, only four motorcades were considered high risk. Those were for President Bill Clinton, Yasser Arafat, head of the Palestine Liberation Organization, Hosni Mubarak, president of Egypt – who was also assigned heavy security because of an alleged assassination attempt in the Middle East months earlier – and President Fidel Castro.

We could clearly see, but not hear, the cars as they passed in front of the loading dock, a parade of police and secret service vehicles, approximately a

12-car motorcade. In addition, although we could not see it, we could hear the loud choppy sound of a helicopter hovering overhead. Later we also learned that there was a police boat stationed right across from the restaurant on the Harlem River near the southbound side of the Major Deegan Expressway. We also heard that the Deegan expressway, a principal traffic highway was temporarily closed, as was Fordham Road, the major street on the south side of the restaurant. While the motorcade was approaching the restaurant and turning into its rear entrance all traffic within the perimeter of the restaurant was stopped.

I was amazed and could not believe what I was witnessing. My mouth was open and I heard Mickey whisper, "Julio, close your mouth, act as if you had done this before" My answer to him: "Can you believe this? All of this is for a Latino." I was literally mesmerized by this overpowering security, something I had never witnessed before in my life. I could not help but think about the fact that all this was for a man that our own country had tried to assassinate on numerous occasions. Yet, while he was here in this country, they were putting all this high-level security in place for him. I wondered if this was the norm or if this was just because this was the South Bronx?

After the parade of police cars and secret service vehicles passed by and the sound of the helicopter slowly began to fade, one lone and long black limousine stopped and began to back up into the loading area of the garage. All three of us stood silently as the black limo continued to back up very slowly to the left side of where we were standing. When the limo came to a halt the secret service agent next to us communicated through the headphone with the agents inside the vehicle, apparently telling them that everything was cleared for President Castro and his entourage to exit the limo. The secret service driver stepped out of the vehicle first, visually checked out the area, looked at all of us standing there and nodded his head. Upon that gesture, another agent opened the back passenger side of the limousine and the Cuban delegation began to exit the vehicle. I recognized Ricardo Alarcón who had been the Cuban Ambassador to the United Nations for many years. I had heard and learned about his eloquence in several speeches that I had read while I was in undergraduate school. I also remembered him from a time in 1971, when he was invited to speak at Queens College. A major disturbance broke out when Cuban exiles protested Alarcon's presence on campus. It was practically a riot and Mickey Melendez, now standing next to me, was a victim of that mêlée when he got burned with acid thrown by the Cuban exile protesters. I was just a freshman at Lehman, but heard and saw pictures of that confrontation, which became a topic of conversation at many of our campuses.

The second person I recognized was then - Cuban Foreign Minister Roberto Robaina. I only knew of him because I had read several articles prior to the visit, which portrayed him as a popular well-dressed individual and highlighted him as a leading member of a younger generation of Cuban leaders.

The third person I recognized was the only woman in the group and she was the last to exit before Fidel. She was Fidel's official translator. I recognized her from the news coverage of Fidel during his time in New York, before he came to the Bronx. In all, there were five, or six people who had exited the limo before – and we still hadn't gotten a glimpse of the guest of honor, Fidel.

# MEETING PRESIDENT FIDEL CASTRO

The last person to step out of the limousine was President Fidel Castro. He stepped out and stood there tall and erect, straightening his tie. I looked at him and was intrigued by the physical size of President Castro. He was much taller in person than he appeared in any of the pictures and film clips I had seen of him. He also had a presence, an energy, something that I had felt only a few times in my life. It was not the feeling you get when you're about to meet, or greet some known celebrity. I had met many of those from top musicians and actors, to politicians and celebrities. I had met and had dinner with Al Gore and his wife, Tipper Gore; I had met Bill Clinton when he was governor and running for president for the first time. I had met my share of well known or so-called "important" people, but this was a different feeling, something I had felt only a few times in my life.

I remember as a teenager having a similar feeling when I got to see and meet Muhammad Ali. I also felt that energy when I first met A. Phillip Randolph and spent a good half hour talking to him and trying to soak up information about the march on Washington that he organized where Martin Luther King delivered his, famous *"I Have a Dream Speech."* I also felt that energy when a good friend, father Roberto González, whom I had not seen in many years since his days at St. Pius Church in the South Bronx, was ordained as the Auxiliary Bishop of Boston. A large group of us travelled to the Boston Cathedral to witness the occasion of seeing a Puerto Rican priest, whom many of us had met on the streets of the South Bronx, being ordained as Auxiliary Bishop in Boston. At the end of the ceremony when the newly ordained Bishop González walked by us in the middle of this huge cathedral full to capacity, he stopped where we were all seated for a quick second and winked at us. I was at the edge of the pew and felt a bit of that tingling energy that I had experienced then, except this time the energy was at a higher level. I felt my heart beating much faster as I looked at Fidel walking towards me, escorted by Bruno Rodríguez.

When he got to where I was standing (now with my mouth closed), Bruno said, *"Comandante, Este es Julio Pabón, el que organizó el evento."* (Comandante, this is Julio Pabón, the person who organized this event). Fidel stretched out both his hands, to shake mine. I slowly raised mine and he grabbed my hand with his two hands. His hands were big, soft and warm. The fact that he shook my hand with both of his surprised me, because that was something that very few people do. I too, had done that, but only on some occasions. It was something my father, who was a *Curandero* (medicine man), had shared with me. He taught me to shake people's hand with my right hand and to cover the person's hand with my left. He would say that the left hand was, *"La mano más cerca al corazón"* (the hand closest to the heart). He told me to shake like that when I wanted to read someone's energy. My father explained that if I wanted to see beyond what my eyes were seeing, then I had to hold someone's hand with both my hands and look into the person's eyes, which he said were the windows to a person's soul. This was kind of freaky because though I on occasion had shaken a few hands this way, no one had ever shaken my hand like that. I was wondering how and why was Fidel shaking my hand like that and looking into my eyes? Did he believe the same spiritual things my father did? While my mind was trying to analyze his simple handshake, it was what he first said to me that really blew my mind and threw me for a complete loop.

Fidel lowered his head to get closer to me as he held onto my hand with both of his and he said, *"Esto no te va a perjudicar a ti,"* (Doing this is not going to harm you).

I could not believe what I just heard and in a way did not really understand what he was asking. Was President Castro caring about me? Never in my career had anyone ever cared about any repercussions my work on an event might have on me. I could not believe he said that to me. It was something that my father who loved me more than life itself would say. I had worked for so many elected officials and top-level executives and had busted my you- know- what, organizing campaigns to help individuals get elected. I had helped many elected officials get major press and community praise. I had taken on major problems affecting our community and no one had ever asked me if any of the work I did would affect me, or my family in any negative way. Here was this man who was always mentioned as a villain among people of my generation. A man who many would equate with something negative and evil, especially taking into account that his presence had caused a real ruckus, first in New York, and now the Bronx. And the first thing out of his mouth when I met him was his expression of concern for my wellbeing. Fidel knew very little about me and I obviously realized I knew less about him, but here he was meeting me for the first time and with a few words he shuttered my brain into thinking, "Who really is Fidel Castro?"

In a way I was also nervous that the protocol that I had expected was being quickly shattered with his words and body language. There were no aides surrounding him and rushing him away from me. On the contrary, he was taking his sweet time with me. When it hit me that he was sincerely preoccupied with my safety, I was puzzled; I was not prepared for that. What I had anticipated was a quick handshake, my greeting him with a few words to the effect of, "Welcome, President Castro," and then his aides moving him on to another setting.

I was a bit nervous and hearing something I never expected to hear from President Castro left me with a temporary loss of words. However, thinking about his concern for me for organizing the event made me blurt out, "*No, yo estoy bien, esta es la Sierra Maestra de Nueva York,*" (No, I'm fine, this is the Sierra Maestra of New York).

When I said that, his eyes widened and he slowly moved his head a slightly backwards and repeated, "*La Sierra Maestra de Nueva York?*" (The Sierra Maestra of New York?). He was probably trying to understand my meaning and why I was comparing the Bronx with the place where the Cuban revolution got its start, where it was organized and where it survived until victory day —the mountains of Cuba known as La Sierra Maestra.

I answered, "Yes", and told him I considered the Bronx and particularly the South Bronx to be, La Sierra Maestra of New York because we had over 100,000 Puerto Ricans living in the area, so I considered this our base.

Fidel gave me a long stare, squinted his eyes slowly, raised his right hand, grabbed and squeezed his beard and slowly repeated, "*Más de 100,000 puertorriqueños?*" (More than 100,000 thousand Puerto Ricans?). He then put his left arm around my shoulders and said, "*Ven, Julio dime, háblame de estos más de 100 mil puertorriqueños,*" (come Julio, tell me, talk to me more about these more 100 thousand Puerto Ricans).

If my mind was blown by the way he introduced himself to me, now I was totally at a loss. Fidel Castro, President of Cuba, leader of a successful revolution in the Caribbean, was walking down this corridor with his hand over my shoulders and asking me about the Puerto Rican community like he was my "home boy"; as if we were close and had known each other for years! I wasn't expecting anything like this from a man whom I just met a few minutes ago and whom I presumed had minimal contact with people outside of his closest circle. It was incredible; it felt like if it was just the two of us in the corridor. There was no one between us, no security, no personal aides, nothing to interrupt our conversation and what appeared to be our impromptu bonding. Yet here I was, a Puerto Rican from the South Bronx, walking wrapped in the arm of President Fidel Castro. My mind was beginning to settle a bit more and I found more words to answer his second question as to who were the Puerto Ricans of the Bronx. However, in the back of my mind, I also could not help but think that there had been so many attempts to assassinate him, supposed this was the perfect location for a hit on him? Suppose Jimmy's Bronx Café in the South Bronx was the perfect location for an assassination and here I was so close to him. I would definitely be a victim as well. The Secret Service could justify that they had warned me to cancel, or move the venue to Manhattan. If something happened, they could blame it on the event being in the Bronx. In those few seconds my mind raced like a man with ADHD on steroids. But I remained calm, as we slowly walked down the corridor, like a father and son strolling through the park. Except that this was not a park. We were in the back area of Jimmy's Bronx Café slowly walking to the double doors that led to the main ballroom where the real activity was to begin.

I calmed myself by thinking of another of my father's wise sayings: "*Todo tiene un propósito,*" (Everything has a purpose). I chilled and began to explain to Fidel that the majority of the Puerto Ricans in the Bronx came from Puerto Rico in "The Great Migration" of the 1950s. I explained many of those who came to New York were like my father, a migrant farm worker. I told him how difficult it was for that generation and the subsequent generations to be accepted in this country and that many members of my generation had been killed as combatants in the numerous wars and or by the violence and drugs of the streets, but with all of that negativity we had still survived. I told him that people of my father's generation had raised children like myself who had survived the streets of the South Bronx and we were "*atrevidos*" (courageous, daring) and that is why we organized the dinner.

I explained that because the Bronx was the borough that was home to the Puerto Rican/Latino majority in the city, it was appropriate for us to welcome him to our dinner. He asked me about those present at the dinner and I said the house was packed. I said we started out with a small number of about 25 guests, but that once word got out about the dinner, the number of people who wanted to attend began to grow to a point that we had to stop inviting guests. I explained that many of our guests were professionals, from all sectors of our community, including teachers, judges, elected officials, musicians, businessmen and businesswomen, and several tradesmen and tradeswomen. I also told him that not everyone present agreed with him, or with the Cuban revolution, because they did not understand it, and that for the most part, many of the guests only knew what the media and our government had been telling us for years. However, I assured President Castro that though everyone present might not agree with him, or support the Cuban revolution, everyone in attendance was respectful of our differences and were present because they too agreed that the actions of our mayor to disinvite him from the dinner for all of the delegates of the United Nations was disrespectful. He listened attentively, but the secret service personnel who were putting themselves in position to open the door so that President Castro could enter the main ballroom interrupted our conversation.

A very unexpected experience, President Castro putting his arm around me and chilling like two homeboys (Photo Personal Archives)

# FIDEL ENTERS THE MAIN BALLROOM:
## THE REACTION WAS SURPRISING

Moments before President Castro entered the main ballroom. (Photo Personal Archives)

The minute the door was opened and the guests got a glimpse of President Castro, they began to applaud. As soon as Fidel entered, I motioned for him and his security to walk him towards the left side of the door, to the vacant table on the left side of the stage that was reserved for him and his entourage. However, when he walked in the guests that were seated at the tables towards the right side of the door, spontaneously jumped to their feet and began to give him a standing ovation. Those closest to the door and to the area where Fidel was walking began to reach over the rope that we set up to cordon off the area where Fidel was to sit, to try and shake hands with Fidel or to touch him.

Congressman José Serrano, President Fidel Castro and Julio Pabón
as they entered main ballroom (Photo Personal Archives)

Fidel was so close, that he noticed the commotion and turned away from the direction of his table and took a few steps towards them, walked over to appease the few people that were reaching out to him. When he shook the hands of the few guests at that table who were closest to him, all the others at that table and others from the surrounding tables also began to stretch out their hands toward him. The rope came loose and the two security agents, one on each side of Fidel, as well as myself, realized Fidel was now moving away from his table and more towards the excited guests with their outstretched hands, as they tried to reach Fidel. It was like Fidel was a Rock Star, walking into a concert hall of groupies. However, what surprised me the most was that some of those coming closer and anxiously stretching their hands were people who had told me that they were attending the event because they disagreed with Mayor Giuliani's disrespectful action of snubbing Fidel, not because they supported President Fidel Castro, or sympathized with the Cuban revolution.

As Fidel walked now past the rope and into the general seating area, the crowd began to swell with more guests wanting to shake Fidel's hand. At that point, I was next to Fidel and going with the flow. I have had experience with security as a lead aide to several elected officials and other political and non-political celebrities. I knew how to maneuver crowds, but this was quite different. Usually my experience was that we walked with the elected officials and introduced him or her to the people so that the elected official could shake hands with different individuals; this was totally the opposite. Here people were swarming over, wanting to shake Fidel's hand without any prompting whatsoever. I looked at Fidel and the two security agents; one was Cuban and the other was American. Fidel looked quite relaxed. He was smiling and his body language was telling me that he was really enjoying the moment. However, the two security agents were far from relaxed. I could sense their anxiety, as their eyes scanned the crowd from left to right looking at everyone who was getting close to Fidel. They were looking at every outstretched and waving hand. At that moment his Cuban security person moved his hands in front of my body, grabbed Fidel by his left elbow, looked at him and nudged him back towards his table in the front. Fidel, put his right hand over the agent's hand, looked at him and calling him by his first name, said, *"Tranquilo, Julio dijo que estamos en la Sierra Maestra"*, (Relax, Julio said we were are in the Sierra Maestra). (I later learned in Cuba while researching for the book that that agent was, Colonel José Delgado who was the head of Fidel's secret service). Fidel then looked at me and smiled. I could not help but also smile and I felt even closer to this man who I had met for the first time just minutes earlier, and who had taken to heart my words about the South Bronx being our Puerto Rican Mecca, our Sierra Maestra.

The fact is that a man who has had more than 600 attempts against his life needs to have more than security easing his mind. While in Cuba researching for this book, I was told by several former and present aides and government officials that one of Fidel's famous quotes regarding his personal security was when he was on a foreign trip preparing to board a plane and he was asked if he was wearing his bulletproof vest. Fidel unbuttoned his shirt to show he did not have one and answered, *"Yo tengo un chaleco moral,"* (I have a moral vest). The quote made me understand that night in 1995 when Fidel put his arm around me and asked about the guests and his lack of hesitation about walking into the crowd. It's as if Fidel has a unique ability to read people and circumstances. My father who was a very spiritual man had always taught me that in order to see, I had to open more than my eyes. He was referring to the other teaching that is rarely taught, on the spiritual side of our existence. He told me to always remember, *"Porque tu no entiendes algo no quiere decir que no existe,"* (Just because you do not understand something does not mean it does not exist). Was it possible that Fidel Castro was also a spiritual person like my father? Perhaps he too understood his connection to the spiritual world, or what many more commonly call the "energy of the universe," and as such was able to feel, read and interpret the energy around him as it was evident to me and many others that President Castro had an energy that was quite present that night in the South Bronx.

Obviously Fidel Castro was not afraid to die because he was not afraid to live. This is the only explanation I can think of for a man to be able to have survived so many attempts on his life and yet live without fear. Fidel had survived the wrath of the most powerful country on earth, whose leaders had wanted him dead.

We all continued our walk in a semi circle back towards the front of the stage, with Fidel shaking more hands than any politician I had ever seen on any campaign trail. As we were winding down to bring Fidel back to his table, Bruno Rodríguez told Fidel about another table where some of his countrymen were sitting. Bruno brought Fidel to the table where Bob Sancho was sitting with his guest. Mr. Sancho was a community leader in El Barrio and the South Bronx also known for organizing some great concerts. Mr. Sancho had brought the great Cuban pianist, Chucho Valdez, leader of the popular Cuban group Irakere and Carlos Emilio Morales, the group's bass player, to the dinner. Bruno introduced Fidel to Bob Sancho and Fidel said: *"Me dicen que tienes a dos de nuestros musicos aqui."* (They tell me that you have two of our musicians here). Fidel smiled and shook hands with both. If anything, that must have made Fidel feel more at home and comfortable. Bob Sancho later told me that after the dinner he commented to Chucho Valdez that he must had met Fidel Castro many times in Cuba. But Chucho told him he had never met Fidel before. Sancho told him, that he would never forget that it was in the South Bronx that he got to meet President Fidel Castro for the first time.

Fidel then finished making his semi rounds of the guest tables nearest the stage. They were all pleasantly surprised by what had just occurred. The applause for Fidel was continuous until he finally sat at his table.

Another musician who really wanted to meet Fidel Castro was Willie Colón, who approached Franklin Flores and pleaded with him to introduce him to Castro. Franklin brought Willie Colón to the guest table where Fidel was sitting. President Castro shook Willie Colón's hand and said, *"Es un honor conocerlo,"* (It's an honor to meet you). Franklin and I wondered later if President Castro really knew Willie Colón was one of our great Latin music icons, or if he was just being super-polite.

I sat at the table with President Fidel Castro and all of the Cuban officials and his translator. I purposely sat across from him with my back to the stage so that I could have a better security angle looking over Fidel's shoulder. He was purposely seated on the chair that had its back to the wall and closest to the door where he had entered the room. Behind him were a number of both Cuban and U.S. secret service agents. Congressman Serrano sat next to President Castro and went over the program that we had printed for the event.

Everyone at the table was excited by the impromptu encounter that obviously was a big hit. It was not just for the guests who got to shake Fidel's hand, but also for members of the Cuban delegation, who, judging by the looks on their faces, were perhaps not expecting their President to have been showered with so much affection from a community which they knew very little. I was sure that both, the Cuban and American secret services were also at ease and glad that the little deviation went well and was over. I looked over to Jerry Fontanez, who was never more than 10 to 15 feet from Fidel and I, always behind the Cuban and U.S. security team, once we entered the ballroom. We made eye contact and Jerry nodded his head and smiled. I could see that he too was relieved that Fidel's unplanned walk through that front area of the ballroom went well with no problems. I later learned from Jerry how uptight his security was trying to stay not more than arm's length from Fidel. It appeared that the unexpected walk into the crowd had stressed everyone except Fidel.

While everyone was settling in, a member of the Cuban secret service made an announcement, outlining strict rules in both English and Spanish. He told the audience that once President Castro began speaking no one would be allowed to stand. If anyone stood they would be immediately removed from the ballroom, without exception. I walked over to Carlos Nazario and told him we could begin whenever he was ready. I was glad that the event was finally going to start and follow the agenda that we had planned. Besides, sitting at a table with Fidel and some of the highest-ranking Cuban officials was not something with which I felt comfortable. I was at a loss for words. My mind was swirling with more thoughts than usual that I wanted to process. I have always been hyper and could easily entertain several thoughts at once. I was multitasking, before the word became popular. However, this went beyond multitasking; this was at another level.

I was still more concerned about security than anything else. I was concerned whether the media that we had admitted to the event would honor our agreement that this was not a media event, but rather a private dinner, and that therefore no questions would be allowed. I was worried whether someone dangerous had infiltrated the capacity crowd with our 300 guests and had somehow slipped through our multilevel security system. I was concerned that the guests that we had invited and who had been approved by both secret service agencies were legit and they too would respect our guest and not blurt out something embarrassing, disrespectful, or try to ask questions, or get up during President Castro's speech. We had identified one agitator and removed her from the dinner; however, I wondered if there were others.

I was pleased that the event was moving swiftly and closer to the final phase. However, I still was not comfortable and kept revisiting my concerns with the U.S. Secret Service and could not help but wonder whether this would be the place to make an attempt on Fidel's life? Was I playing a high-stakes political game by inviting Fidel Castro to the South Bronx? Was my decision to not change locations and insist that the event take place in the South Bronx playing into the hands of an attempt on President Castro's life? I thought a lot about the fact that the dinner was not on President Castro's agenda until a few days earlier. The fact that he was coming to an event and location that no one had thought about, or that was not on anyone's radar prior to his arrival to New York made me think a lot. It was hard to believe that I was now sitting there across from Fidel Castro and soaking in his high energy. I could not help but wonder if I was being played, or if the event was simply going much smoother than I would have thought possible?

My mind was too busy for me to appreciate that I was probably sitting next to the top level of the Cuban leadership, the legendary revolutionaries of my lifetime. Under other more comfortable and relaxing circumstances, I would have cherished the moment. I probably would have been burning our guests' ears, especially Fidel's, with a multitude of questions. As a history major who had been an adjunct professor of history and a social studies teacher, I would have loved to have this circumstance repeated in a different environment. I could easily spend hours talking and outlast any of Fidel's longest speeches with questions, but this was not the case that night. I felt as if this was a party in my house and everything had to go well; that absolutely nothing could go wrong and if it did, everyone would be blaming me. I had too much on my mind to savor the moment.

We all served ourselves more water. I raised my glass in a toast to Fidel. He raised his glass, as so did everyone at our table. Carlos began walking up to the podium to begin the program that everyone was expecting. I was glad that we were about to begin. The sooner the event was over and Fidel was out of the South Bronx, the more comfortable I would be and only then perhaps I could I appreciate what we, a few Puerto Ricans with no major titles or international connections except for Congressman Serrano, had accomplished.

# THE MAIN PROGRAM BEGINS

Carlos Nazario looked over to me to let me know that he was starting the event. He walked over to the podium, adjusted the microphone and began his welcoming remarks. As president of the National Puerto Rican Business Council, he welcomed our guests and the Cuban delegation. He reiterated what the Cuban official had stated about people remaining in their seats while President Castro was speaking. He explained how the council agreed unanimously to sponsor the dinner. He thanked me for bringing up the idea and coordinating the efforts to bring President Castro to the Bronx. He then introduced me as a member of the council and organizer of the event.

I excused myself from the table and walked up to the podium. I stated that we were going to speak in Spanish and that we were not going to need to translate anything because we were in the Bronx. The audience accepted my words with applause. I thanked Carlos for his leadership as president of the National Puerto Rican Business Council, and for having the courage to go ahead with what we all thought was a crazy idea and for allowing me to introduce the idea to the board and leadership of the council. I also thanked Bruno Rodríguez and the members of the Cuban mission to the United Nations for their efforts in working with the National Puerto Rican Business Council. I stated that it was about time that we as Puerto Rican businessmen in the United States began to dialog with our brothers in Cuba. I then welcomed all of the guests and began to explain how the idea of reacting to the mayor's insult was conceived with a phone call from a friend, David Galarza.

I explained how the event was started and organized by a bunch of *"atrevidos"* (bold individuals) who demanded respect as part of New York's Latino community. I explained how we were all *"atrevidos"* for coming to a restaurant that the press had criticized on numerous occasions for being a place of "unsavory characters." I explained how Jimmy Rodríguez, the owner of the restaurant, was an *"atrevido"* for building an upscale quality restaurant in an abandoned lot when no one else in government or private business would dare to invest. I also paid homage to various other *"atrevidos"* who were present; those who fought to transform a factory building in the South Bronx into one of the first bilingual colleges in the United States, Eugenio Maria de Hostos Community College, and to Puerto Rican activists like Richie Perez, Mickey Melendez, Franklin Flores and others who had been involved in the struggle to assure that our community was respected.

I explained how the evening's event was born out of a simple idea of just writing a news release to demonstrate our anger as a Puerto Rican/Latino community over the mayor's insensitivity and lack of respect toward President Fidel Castro.

I detailed how important it was for us as Boricuas (Boricuas is a more progressive/cultural term for Puerto Ricans) to be respected as we had been living in a city that had disrespected many of our elders and many of us much too often, therefore our generation was one that took action to demonstrate that our community had to be respected. I explained that by inviting President Castro to our community, we were demonstrating respect for our community and ourselves. I stated my belief that many other Latino communities throughout the country would also look up to the Puerto Rican community of New York for taking a stand against our mayor's insult and for doing the right thing. I thanked President Fidel Castro and his staff for coming and joked that we never thought that would happen.

I explained that when Congressman Serrano confirmed that President Castro was indeed coming we went from inviting approximately 25 to 30 people to a small dinner to the present crowd that had filled to overflowing the largest banquet hall in Jimmy's Bronx Café. I thanked everyone who supported the idea that we all thought was crazy. I shared my perspective that we had to be *"atrevidos"* to do what we did and told all the guests present that they too were *atrevidos* for daring to come to the dinner despite their possible differences. But I reminded them it was to be expected because the Bronx is a borough of *"atrevidos."*

I then turned to President Castro and told him that if we did not stop adding names to the guest list that we could have easily filled up Yankee Stadium for this event. Everyone laughed including Fidel and those at his table. I continued to look at President Castro and turned a bit more serious. I told him that though I was more than happy to be an *Atrevido* and invite him to come to the Bronx, I had a bone to pick with him because we had some serious differences.

The room went silent. I guess everyone must have been wondering, "Where is Julio going with this? What is Julio about to say?" Mickey Melendez, Franklin Flores, Liz Figueroa and perhaps my daughter, Kimberly, were the only ones not wondering what was about to come out of my mouth because they had heard my speech before, either when I was writing it or after it was translated by Franklin and I had to practice reading it in Spanish.

Fidel became very attentive; he leaned forward as he crossed his hands and placed them on the table and stared at me. I then proceeded to remind him of a recent interview he did with CNN when he was asked whether he wanted the Atlanta Braves or the Cleveland Indians to win the baseball World Series. He had replied the Atlanta Braves. I told him the majority of Puerto Ricans wanted Cleveland to win because there were more Puerto Ricans playing for that team and some of them, like Carlos Baerga and Sandy Alomar, had visited our communities. Everyone burst out laughing including Fidel and his entire entourage. Everyone became more relaxed again; I thanked everyone, all the *Atrevidos* involved for making the dinner happen. I thanked Jimmy Rodríguez for agreeing to let us use his restaurants name in the news release that became the unexpected official invitation, as well as for putting up with the inconveniences involved with securing the restaurant for President Fidel Castro's visit. I then introduced Congressman José Serrano who would present President Fidel Castro to our guests.

Congressman Serrano got up and walked to the podium. He thanked me and delivered an emotional speech emphasizing the historic nature of the evening. He highlighted the fact of this historical moment where Cuba and Puerto Rico were together in the Bronx demonstrating their presence and unity. He said that by our actions, we demonstrated that the Puerto Rican community was not going to permit its behavior to be dictated from Miami or New Jersey. Serrano said the evening presented a perfect opportunity to start a movement to make the United States government end its blockade of Cuba. Serrano reminded everyone that the United States was now trading and had diplomatic relations with Communist China, and also with Vietnam, even though the United States had fought a war against the latter country. His words struck a chord because many young men in his South Bronx district were still suffering from the effects of their exposure to Agent Orange when they were serving in the U.S. military in Vietnam. He stated that perhaps the reason the blockade against Cuba has lasted so long was because of our government leaders' personal dislike of Cuba's leader, a Latino. Serrano wondered out loud if there had been a blockade against a European country, whether it would have been lifted long ago. The crowd burst into a loud applause; the majority understood the subtle racism of the U.S. policy against Cuba and the discrimination that many of us had faced growing up in a city that treated us as foreign immigrants rather than migrants who are American citizens.

Serrano ended his presentation by making an appeal to those present with the following words:

"In this community here this evening is the Boricua political power. From here this evening a political message will go out that this policy by our country (against Cuba) needs to end. Puerto Ricans have the ability to be the American citizen that has the corresponding obligation to educate our great nation on its behavior in Latin America, in our Caribbean. We here tonight can start something new regarding this behavior as part of this daring act, a movement that this treatment against Cuba has to end."

Serrano described himself as an American citizen, a patriot who served in the U.S. armed forces and who defended this country. But he said a true patriot is that one that tells his government when the government is wrong and urges them to change. And that's what Serrano was doing.

He received a long round of applause and began to introduced President Castro, saying, "For me it is an honor and a pleasure to present our invitee who accepted our invitation to come to the Bronx, with respect above all to the people of Cuba, we give our warm welcome to President Fidel Castro." The audience began to chant *"Fidel Amigo, El Pueblo Está Contigo,"* (Fidel friend, the people are with you) and *"Cuba Si Bloqueo No,"* (Cuba Yes, Blockade No) for a very long minute.

# FIDEL IS PRESENTED WITH GIFTS

Bronx youth welcoming President Fidel Castro. (Photo Personal Archives)

The chants went on as President Castro got up from our table and walked slowly over to the stage. He stopped halfway to the podium and just looked into the crowd, smiling and humbly taking in the incredible spontaneous love and respect coming from all of u giving him a standing ovation. Perhaps even he was feeling a bit overwhelmed by the reaction that he was receiving from people attending an event that was not on his political agenda. He had only decided to attend our dinner 72 hours earlier when he learned of the invitation from Fernando Remírez, his representative in Washington D.C., and decided to come, despite the counsel of his advisors and the U.S. Secret Service not to do it. It was like watching a man who was appreciating the audience without words. His smile and body language was giving out a glow that was felt by everyone in the audience, an unspoken statement of a man who was validating a decision that he had made and that perhaps only he understood. Looking back after concluding the research I did for this book, I can understand now more than I did then on that evening and the particular warmth that President Castro gave off. Almost everyone I interviewed, both in Cuba and here in the states had mentioned it. It is warmth that comes from a person who is centered and is at one with his true spirit and conviction of purpose. He made a decision to come to the South Bronx and it was obviously the correct decision for him; the kind of spontaneous decisions that only certain leaders have the ability to make.

The applause and chants were just as loud and long as when we first opened the doors and he first appeared into the dining hall. He approached the podium ready to speak. However, before he began he was told that we had a special presentation by three youths. Fidel was pleasantly surprised, he threw up his hands, stepped away from the podium and watched as Elena Flores (who was Nancy and Franklin's daughter), Vanessa Ramos (she was the daughter of Susana Ríos, my special assistant), and Julio Antonio Pabón (my son) walked on the stage. Each had a gift for him.

Elena was first and she gave President Castro a bouquet of one dozen white roses. Elena became so emotional upon handing the flowers to Fidel that she began to cry. Fidel comforted her by embracing and kissing her on her forehead. He put his arm around her and Elena was comforted and looked as relaxed as if a loving grandfather was holding her. They posed for photographers who were taking pictures of Fidel's every move. Many of the guests were touched and surprised by Fidel's warm and impulsive spontaneous reaction to Elena's tears. They began to chant "Cuba, Cuba Cuba, *Puerto Rico te Saluda*" (Cuba, Puerto Rico Salutes you). Elena was now calm and asked Fidel if he could autograph a copy of the program. Fidel put the flowers under his left forearm and signed the program for her.

When Elena finished, Vanessa Ramos walked over to Fidel and gave him two Latino Sports baseball caps. Vanessa was poised and did not look nervous, though she told me when I interviewed her for the book that all the flashes from the photographers' cameras overwhelmed her. The hats I chose were green and red, and I had personally chosen those two colors from the many colors that we had in the office. I had recently ordered the hats to begin a marketing campaign to promote Latino Sports. I thought that if Fidel wore one of my hats and that picture was made public, it would help promote my new line of Latino Sports apparel better than a picture showing any baseball player wearing my hat. I remember thinking that I wanted to choose colors Fidel might like. I choose green because I knew Fidel liked wearing his olive green military fatigues, and of course, red, which is the color associated with revolution. For those who follow the Afro-Cuban Santeria religion, red also represents the African God, Chango. I was trying to cover all the angles with those two hats.

Fidel took the hats, studied them for a quick second and smiled. I was praying for him to try one on, but he did not. I thought, "Well, "at least I tried."

Fidel thanked Vanessa and shook her hand. He posed with Vanessa for a few more pictures and then Vanessa stepped back as Julio Antonio approached the podium.

Julio Antonio was the oldest of the three, at age 15, and as he had been doing since he was a small child, he was rolling with the scene. He appeared very comfortable and looked the part. He had a white shirt with a colorful tie and acted as if he had rehearsed his part on stage with President Castro. Julio presented Fidel with a huge oversized red boxing glove that had been donated by Dante Ortiz, a Boricua business owner who had his office across from me on 149th Street. Dante made trophies, plaques and some apparel for boxers and had contacted me the minute he heard that Fidel was coming to the Bronx. He told me that he would like to donate a gift, a large boxing glove to give to President Fidel Castro.

He told me what he printed on the glove: **FIDEL # 1 Bronx, NY • DANTE • Oct. 23, 1995**.

I remembered thinking and considering Dante's proposal. Many people who wanted to give a gift to Fidel had offered us many other gifts, and I could not possibly accept every one of them. However, I liked the idea of a boxing glove for Fidel, a man who has been a revolutionary guerrilla fighter and fighting for Cuba since the triumph of the revolution. I thought that the glove was a good addition to the gifts we had already planned; it was unique and quite appropriate. I thanked Dante for his generosity and thoughtfulness.

When Julio Antonio handed the glove to President Castro, Castro leaned back and put on a huge smile. He gave the hats to Julio Antonio to hold and he took the glove from Julio. Fidel raised the glove to his eyesight and looked inside (I smiled and thought, "Always security conscious"), he then placed his left hand into the glove. The smile that I saw on Fidel Castro's face was one of those smiles when someone is truly enjoying the moment, one of pure appreciation and pleasure. It was obvious that President Castro really enjoyed that gift. He pounded the glove with his right hand as a boxer would do and then threw a left jab and raised the glove up above his head as a championship boxer raises his hand when he is victorious in a fight. It was obvious that Fidel was touched by the gift's creativity and he really enjoyed it. The audience loved it as well and again broke out in loud applause, accompanied by chants. Several yelled out, "*Dale Duro Fidel*," (Hit them hard Fidel). The media went into a picture-taking fury. They asked Fidel to pose and he obliged and again the flashes were everywhere. Julio was in the middle of that limelight and was taking it like a trooper. His smile also demonstrated that he too was enjoying the moment. He posed with Fidel for several shots. Fidel removed the glove and gave it to his translator standing behind Julio. President Castro and Julio shook hands. Castro smiled and patted Julio on his head as he stepped away.[xiii]

I smiled and was grateful to Dante for convincing me to allow his gift to be given to President Castro. I felt that we scored a knockout with that gift.

15 year-old, Julio Antonio Pabón after handing President Castro the oversized boxing glove (Photo Personal Archives)

# FIDEL DELIVERS A SHORT, BUT IMPACTFUL SPEECH

After the presentation of the gifts, President Castro walked to the podium. He straightened his tie and stepped away for a quick second as the stage was being cleared. He addressed some of the people who were standing in front of the stage, one of whom apparently had made a comment, or asked a question. It was obvious that President Castro was feeling comfortable in our surroundings. When the stage was finally cleared, Fidel dismissed the guest in front of the stage by clasping both his hands. It was like acknowledging the guest with his gesture and saying "thank you, or you're welcome." He walked to the front of the podium, placed his left hand over the left side of his face as if he was trying to focus and get back to the official part of the dinner, to address the members of the National Puerto Rican Business Council and our guests. Once at the podium, he slowly adjusted the microphones for his height. He stood there for a quick second staring out towards the audience, squinting his eyes, and perhaps adjusting his vision to the darkened room and the lights from the news photographers and camera crews positioned about forty or fifty feet in front of him. Once again the audience began chanting, "Fidel, Fidel" and once again President Castro looked pleasantly overwhelmed by the loving reception he was experiencing in this impromptu dinner in the South Bronx.

President Castro received a loving welcome from the guests
at Jimmy's Bronx Café. (Photo Personal archives).

President Fidel Castro addressing the audience at Jimmy's
Bronx Café. (Photo Personal Archives)

When the chanting stopped President Castro stood tall, cleared his throat
and started his speech saying: *"Queridos amigos y distinguidos atrevidos,"*
(Dear friends and distinguished daring/bold ones). The crowd immediately

broke out in a loud cheer and applause, including myself. I personally felt proud that he understood the essence of my presentation and quoted the title of my speech, "*Atrevidos*." He obviously took in everything I had explained to him when we walked together from the garage loading dock to the banquet hall as well as what I said in my presentation. In his opening remarks, those first few words made me feel that he totally understood that we were "*atrevidos*," — daring and courageous Puerto Ricans. His words were directed not just at those of us who wrote the initial news release that snowballed into the actual invitation and the event then taking place, but also to everyone who helped organize and dared to attend. The majority of the guests were businesspeople, and professionals who probably would be chastised and criticized by business associates, co-workers, neighbors, and even family members for attending a dinner with President Fidel Castro.

He then began speaking in a very slow and methodical way using his facial expressions and hands to highlight or emphasize a point. President Castro had been known for being a very charismatic speaker and he was demonstrating those attributes to many who had never seen or heard him speak. Everyone was quiet and attentive, glued to President Castro's every word and expression. Many told me afterwards that they felt like freshmen students in a college history course with a distinguished professor.

He stated that if they noticed that he had a problem seeing, it was because of the modern era that we were living in and the glare of so many strong lights.

He continued, and mentioning me by name, said that I told him we might have had to have the dinner at the baseball stadium (because of the number of guests that wanted to attend but could not). Fidel said, "*pero a mi me parece estar viendo aquí un estadio en este magnífico "'room'" de Jimmy que ha sido tan atrevido y tan valiente como para prestarlo esta noche,*" (It appears to me that I am seeing a stadium here in this magnificent "room" that Jimmy has been so courageous and valiant to lend for this evening). The audience broke out in laughter and applause.

President Castro went on to speak and mentioned how impressed and moved he and the members of the Cuban delegation were by our words and actions. He spoke of the many things that unite us, including Spanish, our shared common language. It was humbling to hear President Castro mention my name a second time when he stated: *"Realmente, me han impresionado las palabras de Julio Pabón y José Serrano. Me ha gustado muchísimo la forma sencilla, directa, clara, y franca con que hablaban; además saben lo que dicen, y dicen mucho, y lo dicen con todo el cuidado necesario,* (Really, I have been impressed by the words of Julio Pabón and José Serrano. I really enjoyed the simple, direct, clear and frank way they spoke; besides, they know what they are saying and they are saying a lot and they say it with all the necessary care."

At this point, President Fidel Castro captivated me, too. I felt like a student again and for the first time forgot about the security issues and became immersed in each of his words, facial expressions and mannerisms.

I have had the privilege of seeing quite a number of national and world-renowned speakers and I have watched others on video, but hearing President Fidel Castro speak especially in the warm and welcoming atmosphere that we created in Jimmy's Bronx Café was unique and special. Of course, I had heard President Castro speak on recordings and on video. However, watching him in person and up close that evening was something quite special. *El Diario* reporter, Gerson Borrero stated it best in an article he later wrote: "Fidel's Visit Was a Home Run," where he stated: "Fidel has a charisma...a captivating style...that can seduce you."

After he spoke about the genuine emotional feeling that he and his delegation were experiencing, he went on to clarify and apologize for choosing the Atlanta Braves over the Cleveland Indians in the World Series. He said, *"Me parece que antes de continuar, debo de aclarar este serio problema de las Grandes ligas, porque ya veo que ustedes están con Cleveland..."* (I believe that before I continue I should clear this serious problem of the Major Leagues because I see how you are with Cleveland). Everyone again broke out in laughter.

He continued to give an explanation as to how the one thing many North Americans know about him is that he loves baseball. He clarified that he also likes other sports, but that every North American who visits him gives him gifts; a baseball, a bat, or a book that may be a biography of some famous baseball player, or one with baseball statistics. He stated that he had received so many baseball gifts that he could easily create a baseball museum. Again the audience broke out in laughter.

President Castro explained that during the visit he was doing a television interview and he was asked whom he favored in the World Series. He said that question was not nice, and again everyone laughed. He explained how he had been traveling through several Latin American countries prior to coming to the United States, visiting en route Uruguay for a summit of Latin American heads of state. He said that he had no time to read any cables or newspapers, because "it was just speeches upon more speeches." He clarified that they were not his speeches, but those of other heads of state. He joked and stated that with his speeches at least he is entertained, but with the others he got bored. Again, the audience laughed and applauded him. It was apparent that President Castro was really relaxed and enjoying himself as much as the audience was enjoying his sense of humor and the details he provided.

He went on to explain that he now held the record for giving the shortest speech in that summit. He told the audience that the time limit for the speeches was for five, not more than six minutes, and his presentation was three minutes; something he described as a record of all records. He had the audience in stitches. It appeared to many that this so called "vicious dictator" (as described by some Cuban exiles), who had been disinvited from the heads of state dinner that had been offered by Mayor Giuliani, was having the time of his life with a community that was totally enjoying listening to his anecdotes here in the South Bronx.

President Castro continued by saying that since he was not up to date on the latest baseball developments in the United States, when he was asked which team he favored, he remembered saying, "Well since I am a friend of Ted Turner I have to be for the Braves." But then he continued, that if he had "known that you here in the Bronx are with Cleveland, I would've said, "'look, don't get me into this problem.'" Again the audience burst out in laughter.

As I looked around the room, I saw many of my friends who appeared to be really enjoying the evening and President Castro's presentation, despite their doubts about Fidel Castro and Cuba. If there had been any tension before among any of our guests, it seemed to have disappeared once President Castro began speaking. Their doubts appeared to vanish, melted away by the sincerity, humility, humor, and presence of President Castro speaking from the heart. He reiterated how moved he was to have learned just how many Puerto Ricans were living in the Bronx, along with Dominicans and other Cubans. Then just at that moment, a single voice yelled out, "Uruguayo" (Uruguayan). Fidel stopped, smiled and repeated, "Uruguayo." He said this was a lesson for him and his delegation, since before this day they did not understand that dimension of the Bronx with its diverse Latino population, and now they understood that they had so many brothers among us.

Fidel went on to speak about Cuban and American history, educating many of us about the historical links between Cuba and the United States that included past migrations up to those of the present day. For example many of us, including myself, were unaware that many Cubans came here and fought for America's independence, during the time of George Washington. President Castro told us about that.

He also explained how in the period prior to the Civil War, the Spaniards controlled commerce, the administration and the military in Cuba and the Cubans owned the lands, along with 300,000 slaves. He spoke about how that situation created an annexationist movement in Cuba and how at the time, sectors in both the North and the South in the U.S., favored that movement, thinking they would have two additional votes in the U.S. Senate for their cause.

President Castro was sounding like a professor and an educator on the history of Cuba and the United States. He continued to give a very detailed description of the immigration of Cubans to the United States and how that immigration developed and increased right after the Cuban revolution for very political reasons.

He then went on to explain about the Cuban revolution and put into context many of the criticisms that have been made of Cuba. He said he had read about revolutions and about history and that he believed that the most generous revolution that has existed has been the Cuban revolution.

He also spoke of the Bay of Pigs invasion and the Cubans' capture of 1,300 prisoners, emphasizing how there was not one who received any injury after being captured, not even being hit with a rifle butt. He said this was in keeping with the principles of the Revolution, maintained throughout their war of liberation. He explained that although there were hundreds of casualties on their side, he urged anyone to ask those that were captured in the Bay of Pigs if anyone had even pulled their hair (the audience erupted in laughter).

He stated: "A lie, an exaggeration, repeated once, a thousand, or a million times can never be converted into the truth. A lie no matter how many chose to believe it can never be converted into a truth." The audience again broke out in thunderous applause. It was obvious our guests could relate to much of what President Castro was saying, not because they were leftist, but because they had experienced some form of discrimination, abuse, or lies themselves. Everyone there could relate to Fidel's statement "a lie can not be converted into truth no matter how many times it was repeated." That's because most of us present had climbed the social ladder and had gotten to where we are were by jumping hoops and avoiding all types of obstacles and lies perpetrated against us. Very few guests at the dinner, even if somewhat successful, were born or raised in circumstances of privilege. We each had our own negative encounters, or family related stories of what it was like growing up and surviving in the cement jungle of New York. We had all experienced, or had a close family member who had experienced some form of abuse from a police officer, an employer, or a landlord. That is why I believed that many in the audience were connecting with President Castro's words.

President Castro went on to explain that Cuban ingenuity had made it possible to survive the Cold War and some of the worst periods imaginable. He spoke about how there were still more American cars in Cuba from the 1940s, 1950s and 1960s than in New York, where there were more Japanese cars than any other type (the audience laughed and applauded).

He spoke about the effects of the U.S. economic embargo that he defined as more of an economic blockade. He explained how that blockade prohibits selling Cuba something as simple as aspirins. He mentioned the number of Cubans who had died because they could not get medicines that were available to save their lives, but not sold to Cuba.

He then spoke about Cuba's commitment to helping others. He told of how Cuba has sent over 15,000 doctors to Third World countries; how they sent 2,000 teachers to teach in the mountains of Nicaragua; and how they donated 100,000 pints of blood in ten days to Perú when that country suffered from a devastating earthquake. They also donated 50,000 pints of blood to Armenia and also to Iran when they suffered their catastrophes. They had also donated to several countries in Latin American even though they had no diplomatic relations with them. He said these were the sentiments of humanity and of solidarity that came from the Revolution and that has educated the Cuban people. President Castro concluded by once again thanking Congressman Serrano and me for the words we expressed and by sharing his appreciation for the atmosphere and the ambience of the event, as well as his gratitude that he said he was expressing in the name of the Cuban people.

President Castro saved his deepest emotional feeling for the end when he raised his voice to express his belief that we were all going to be much stronger after this meeting. He lifted both his hands to emphasize his point, raised his voice, and said, "I am sure, absolutely sure that you will be stronger after this meeting. So, rather we should all be proud, you and us. We, for having the honors, with the encouragement of men and women as excellent as you, and you, because you are the ones that make the good causes triumph, because you are just, because you are courageous, because you are noble, because you are generous, because you are in solidarity."

I saw many in the front tables jump to their feet and began to applaud fast and loud. Within seconds the entire audience in the banquet room was standing, whistling and giving President Fidel Castro a resounding and long-lasting ovation, chanting Viva Fidel, Fidel!

# POST PRIVATE RECEPTION WITH FIDEL

As people emptied the banquet hall, Fidel and his entourage were taken to a private special VIP reception organized separately by the owner of the restaurant, Jimmy Rodríguez. The reception was in another smaller room outside the large banquet hall.

There was still a lot of energy in the banquet hall and people were taking their time exiting. Just about everyone was still mesmerized by what they had experienced. Perhaps everyone knew that they had just witnessed a bit of history, and sensed that they had experienced something they would remember for the rest of their lives. They felt the excitement and energy. They knew they would never forget the day when they got to see and hear President Fidel Castro of Cuba for the first time. The impact of what had just occurred was slowly sinking in; many people knew that they had experienced something that was indeed historic. Fidel Castro in the South Bronx, Wow!

Many guests were congratulating me, or thanking me for inviting them. I was pleased, but not ready to chat with anyone as my attention was still on security. I was excited that the event was such a success and that everyone I spoke with was so excited about having been present. I was also pleased that the main event was over and without any problems. However, President

Castro was still in the building and my mind was not going to relax until he was out of the building and on his way back to Manhattan. I wanted to go to the smaller reception, but knew that I could not attend until most of the guests were out of the banquet hall and out of the building. I was not going to be relaxed until the event was officially over and President Fidel Castro was once again exclusively in the hands of the U.S. Secret Service.

Of all the guests who approached me, there is one I cannot forget, George Carva. George was a freelance photographer who was always present at most of the events that pertained to the Puerto Rican community. If he liked you, he would also do your horoscope. George approached me and gave me a glass wrapped in one of the white cloth napkins that were at each table. He told me that this was the glass that Fidel had used to drink water, that it still had his fingerprints that were clearly visible. He said, "Julio, you should keep this." I thanked him, I put the glass down on the table where I was standing, and continued speaking to guests that were leaving. I was also thinking of Fidel and his security and trying to see if he was already in the private room.

I said goodbye to the remainder of the guests that had been milling around and left for the private reception. Halfway there I realized that I had left the glass that George Carva had given me. I immediately returned to the table, but the glass was gone. I was more disappointed than angry, as I could not believe that someone took that glass. There were no service personnel cleaning and none of the tables had yet been cleared, so I believed that it had to have been taken by someone who overheard George Carva when he handed me the glass. So I shrugged and thought "*Era* Nice," as I have been known to say when I lost something important. I put the glass incident behind me and headed off for the private reception.

On my way there I found Jerry Fontanez and his crew and thanked them for their excellent job with security. I invited them to the private reception, but I don't think any of them went, as they were probably more interested in getting home as it was now nearing midnight.

When I arrived at the reception, I saw members of the secret service by the door. You had to have a red tag to enter, or come in with someone who had a red tag. Jimmy went all out and had commissioned a cake that was a replica of the White House to cut for the occasion. At first I could not understand the symbolism of a White House cake for a reception for Fidel Castro. I later learned that the Cuban Capital building was modeled after the U.S. Capitol building in Washington and the Pantheon in Paris.

Jimmy knew that President Castro was a baseball fan and gave him a very unique gift, a collection of three autographed baseballs signed by the three star center fielders of the three New York teams: The balls were autographed by Mickey Mantle of the New York Yankees, Willie Mays of the New York Giants, and Duke Snyder of the Brooklyn Dodgers. Fidel was pleased and surprised, but said it was too much for him to accept knowing how much that might have meant to a New York baseball fan. However, he did accept and said that he would cherish the gift. Jimmy also gave him a baseball jersey with the NY Yankees logo in the front and the name Castro and #1 on the back. It was a funny contradiction to give President Castro a jersey from a team named, the Yankees, given the connotation that word has had in Latin America outside of baseball. Fidel and all those present laughed as he examined the shirt with his name on the back.

After the short presentation of Jimmy's gifts and the cutting of the cake, people began to mingle and network. At that moment I got the book that Mickey had given me, *History Will Absolve Me.* I asked President Castro if he would do me the favor and autograph my book. He looked at the book, smiled and wrote, *"Para mi amigo Julio. De un atrevido a otro."* (To my friend Julio, from one daring one to another). After he signed my book I introduced him to the three women with me; my wife, Liz Figueroa, my daughter, Kimberly, and Susana Rios, my special assistant at my interpreting company, Morivivi Language Services and the mother of Vanessa Ramos, the young girl that gave Fidel the Latino Sports hats. When I introduced Liz, Fidel reached out and kissed her on the cheek. He then smiled, shook the women's hands, and said,

*"Que muchas flores lindas hay en el Bronx,"* (What many beautiful flowers you have here in the Bronx). Liz elbowed me and whispered, *"Miralo, tirando piropos"* (look at him, he's flirting). The ladies loved it and I could see that Fidel's remark instantly broke the ice. He made them feel comfortable and warm. I smiled as well and thought how down to earth President Fidel Castro was. I realized that underneath the title, prestige and power, President Fidel Castro was as much a Latino as any one of us, and as a true Latino was candid in expressing his feelings.

Julio Pabón, Susanna Rios (co-worker), President Castro, Julio Jr, Kimberly Pabón, Liz Figueroa & Carlos Nazario, President of the NPRBC. (Photo Personal Archives)

The ladies wanted to take a picture with Fidel and I looked to see if anyone had a camera. None of us had one, and unfortunately I saw none of the numerous photographers that were in the main ballroom. In those days we did not have smart phones with cameras. I then noticed that Ellen Toscano, Congressman Serrano's special counsel and chief of staff, had a camera and was taking photographs at the other end of the room. I tried calling out to Ellen, but she could not hear me. Fidel noticed our difficulty in getting Ellen's attention and he told a member of the Cuban entourage who was a photographer to take our pictures and to make sure that we got copies of the photographs. We took a few photographs and everyone was elated that we had taken personal photos with President Fidel Castro. Unfortunately, we never did receive the photographs. While interviewing all three ladies for this book, they each remembered and asked if we had ever received the pictures?[xiv]

The private reception was finally coming to an end. My family and others had already left, as the next day was a school and regular workday. It was past midnight and someone yelled out that it was now officially Tuesday and Congressman José Serrano's birthday. We sang a birthday song and congratulated Serrano and soon afterward President Castro and his entourage departed. I was one of the last to leave the building and when I walked outside, I could not help but notice how quiet it was. I had parked by the back of the restaurant and as I walked I saw no police cars, no secret service, no reporters, no protestors, no one. The block was dark, quiet, and once again looking like the South Bronx that I knew. Except that the South Bronx I knew was changed. We just had a famous world known leader visit and his presence in our neighborhood would add to the history of our borough. Before I got into my car, I turned and looked at the building housing Jimmy's Bronx Café and felt extremely proud of what a small group of Puerto Ricans had done bringing attention to the most neglected borough in the greatest city in the world. I could not help but think of one of my favorite quotes by Margaret Mead: "Never doubt that a small group of thoughtful, committed people can change the world, indeed, it is the only thing that ever has." I smiled all the way home knowing we made history.

# EVENT IS FINALLY OVER – THE DAY AFTER

I had told most of my contacts, friends, and clients that I was going to close the office the day after the dinner because we needed a day to recoup. I gave Kimberly a well-deserved day off. However, the real reason was that I did not know what to expect in the aftermath of the Fidel visit. I was not willing to risk having my daughter and I in the office and have some type of negative fallout take place where I worked.

However, I knew that I would have to go to the office to try and get back to my regular normal work schedule. "Normal" was something that was a bit foreign after just spending the last three days in a whirlwind of events that literally took my entire family and me by surprise.

I arrived at the office super early, locked the door and took no calls, only those to my cellular phone. I could also monitor incoming calls on our answering machine. I knew that I had to catch up with a lot of work and did not want any interruptions. I had a pile of phone messages and a tray that read, "Incoming Correspondence" that was full of letters and bills that Kimberly had organized for me that needed my immediate attention.

The last three days were so crazy that it kept me from doing anything related to my businesses, or my personal life. I had totally focused on the Fidel visit and put everything else to the side. I also had a pending trip to Puerto Rico that was like a gift from heaven. I had scheduled that business trip several months earlier, before I knew anything about organizing a dinner for President Fidel Castro, and it could not have come at a better time. An escape from New York two days after the Fidel Castro visit was exactly what I needed to get my mind back to my "business as usual." My mother had always counseled me that it was important to "*cruzar mar*" (cross the ocean) once in a while to free the mind and strengthen the spirit. Crossing over large bodies of water were considered good energy that could help both body and soul. Though I did not understand many of my parents' *consejos* or the advice they gave me at the time, I was always respectful and listened. I knew that they always had meanings that I was not prepared, or ready to understand, but were somehow always on target. My father's saying that "because you do not understand something does not mean that it did not exist" was constantly put to the test in my family. My parents and I were from Guayama, a town known in Puerto Rico as, "*El pueblo de los Brujos*," (The town of witches) and both my parents were into some form of spiritualism. My mother focused on dreams that for the most part always had a meaning. My father was a *curandero* (medicine man) and many people came to see him at our apartment for cures. People would not go to the hospital (there were no doctors' offices in our neighborhood) but came to my father looking for home remedies that seemed to work.

However, before leaving for Puerto Rico, I had to take care of business. By mid-morning I had returned many of the phone calls and gone through much of the mail. Many of the phone calls I made were apologies on my part for not returning the phone calls sooner. I have always had a policy to return phone calls as soon as I could and usually within 24 hours. However, some of those phone calls were from people that had called me days earlier.

Many of the calls were from people who had wanted to either get tickets to attend the dinner with President Fidel Castro, or wanted more information on the event. There were some calls from people congratulating us for having the dinner and there were a few from people who were basically wishing me harm. But I never heard those negative calls in details, because by the first or second word I already knew where their conversation was heading, and I would tell them, *gracias* (thank you) and hang up.

One of the calls was from a reporter from the NY 1 television network inviting me to their Manhattan studios for a live taping on the Fidel Castro visit to the Bronx that would occur early that evening. They explained that they had confirmed Herman Badillo, who at the time had been working with the Giuliani administration. Badillo was a prominent and well-respected Puerto Rican official who was not at our dinner. Since he worked with Giuliani, I was sure he was going to speak against the Castro visit to the Bronx. They asked if I would be willing to appear and talk about our invitation to President Fidel Castro. I said yes. I then called Franklin Flores, who encouraged me to do the show and agreed to go with me.

I also received a phone call from Bruno Rodríguez at the Cuban Mission who asked if I would be willing to be interviewed for Cuban television. I told him I had no problem doing this, he said the crew would contact me directly and that they would probably want to do it in the early afternoon. He also told me that they would be willing to come up to the Bronx and film at my office. My idea of hiding in the office to try and have a "back to normal day" was not happening. By noon, I called our local restaurant for lunch delivery and turned my attention back to the mail, memos, and messages on my desk and on the answering machine. I was determined to try and finish off as much as possible before the Cuban television crew arrived later in the afternoon.

# AN UNEXPECTED VISIT AND GIFT

Being alone in the office was a great idea as I was on a roll and could see that I could be finished with most of the pressing paperwork by the end of the day. I had some proposals that I was working on, but those had no immediate rush and I knew I could take those with me and begin working on them on my plane trip, and complete them in Puerto Rico.

Just before noon someone knocked on the door. I figured they had sent my lunch up earlier than I expected. I walked over to the door, and still thinking about security, opened it with the chain latch on to confirm it was my lunch. When I opened the door, my heart raced a bit when I saw a man standing there with a package wrapped in a brown paper bag under his arm. He must have seen my hesitation and immediately told me he was delivering a gift from *El Comandante*. His profoundly Cuban accent convinced me that he was Cuban, and he also showed me identification from the Cuban Mission.

I took the chain off the door and let him in. He did not want to sit and told me that he just wanted to deliver the package from *El Comandante*. I took the package and inside was a very attractive tan wooden box of Cuban Cohiba cigars. The cigar box was accompanied by a business card from President Fidel

Castro. I was pleasantly surprised and more surprised with the business card, which I immediately put in my wallet.

I thanked my Cuban visitor and told him to please relay my heartfelt appreciation for the box of cigars. I did not smoke; however, I made many friends in New York and Puerto Rico quite happy when I gave them a real quality Cuban cigar that was sent to me by the President of the Republic of Cuba himself.

# CUBAN TELEVISION IN THE STREETS
## OF THE SOUTH BRONX

By the time the Cuban television crew arrived, I had already eaten lunch and had only a few more items to finish in the office. I also wanted to prepare a little for the interview with News 1 that evening, but I figured that was not going to be difficult as I was just going to talk about what we had been stating all along. Our position had always been that when the mayor disinvited President Fidel Castro from his dinner, we in the Puerto Rican community felt that was disrespectful, and decided to invite him to come to a dinner in the Bronx.

When the Cuban reporter and crew arrived at my office, we first engaged in some small talk. The crew was composed of three men who began to prepare me for the interview, by telling me that many people in Cuba were interested to learn how and why the dinner was planned. Apparently, Cuban television was reporting much of their Presidents meetings and encounters in New York and they were really interested in the dinner that had taken place in the South Bronx. Again, unbeknownst to me and to all of us who worked on the dinner, our impromptu event and its sudden appearance on Fidel's schedule took many by surprise. Including people in Cuba. Before President Castro had arrived in New York, his entire schedule had already been planned. Every meeting he had was approved prior to his arrival. Fidel had been invited to many more meetings than the ones that he attended during his visit to New York. President Castro had received over 200 invitations. It was impossible for the Cuban delegation to have accepted the numerous invitations they had received for Fidel. President Castro had also received an invitation from New York's Cardinal O'Connor that they could not schedule. The Cardinal had visited Cuba and met with President Castro months before and perhaps that's why meeting with the Cardinal again while in New York with so many other invitations pending was not a priority.[xv]

President Castro also had received countless requests from the media for exclusive interviews.

The interviews and visits that were scheduled for President Castro were obviously chosen for political reasons and again, it was understandable that the invitations they received from the media were given high priority. That is why Fidel gave interviews to CNN, NBC, CBS, ABC, The New York Times and a local Univision channel from Miami. It was Fidel Castro all over New York. If mayor Giuliani and the Cuban right-wing exile community thought that they were going to embarrass President Castro and the Cuban delegation in the New York media and keep them out of any limelight, they were mistaken. They must have been kicking themselves in the rear because all their tactics backfired and if anything Fidel was getting all the publicity of a celebrity. If Mayor Giuliani was in the newspapers attacking President Castro almost daily prior to his arrival, once Fidel arrived, the news coverage was just the opposite. President Castro was getting more coverage than any other world leader. New York was indeed going through *Fidelmania*.

President Castro also had a lunch at the home of Mortimer Zuckerman, (publisher) of the *Daily News* and a luncheon with numerous business executives on Wall Street organized by David Rockefeller. All the news stations covered Fidel's visit and every night there was a blurb on President's Castro visiting somewhere, or of a demonstration related to his visit. This was also true of the daily newspapers, where he appeared on the front pages on more than one occasion. There was news coverage on President Castro, or about some protest or rally against or in his favor, in the media every day. President Fidel Castro's visit created a media frenzy. The fact that the National Cuban American Foundation was pumping a lot of money into doing everything possible to embarrass the Cuban President during his visit, or use the opportunity to promote their hatred of him and of the Cuban revolution, created the crazy atmosphere that brought more coverage during President's Castro's visit.

President Fidel Castro was the hottest and most popular person during that week in October in New York and everybody wanted a piece of him.

Therefore, our event in the Bronx, where President Castro had attended a dinner, was quite important. Although it was a last-minute event that was only planned and executed in a matter of days, it was of interest to many, especially in Cuba. Cubans were watching and following President Castro's every move in New York as if it was an international baseball game where the Cuban national team was playing for a world championship against the United States, or a championship-boxing match between the U.S. and Cuba. In a way it all felt exactly like a match between those who wanted to portray President Fidel Castro as Mayor Giuliani described him — "a vicious dictator, an avowed enemy of my country." On the other side were the countless numbers of people and organizations who turned out to support President Castro and Cuba's policy of Internationalism helping so many Third World countries. Then there were a number of other people who just wanted to get a glimpse of him. That is why the most respected news organizations and notable citizens of the city were inviting him to their homes and corporate boardrooms for a meeting.

Whatever money was being spent by organizations like the Cuban American Foundation in New York and as vicious as the mayor's statements were, if indeed this had been a baseball game, or a boxing match, it seemed President Fidel Castro was pitching a no-hitter and scoring a knockout.

After the Cuban news crew explained what they wanted to do and we talked about the issues related to the visit, we agreed that the best place to do the interview would be on the streets of the South Bronx.

We went outside and walked from my office on 149th Street to Third Avenue. This area is one of the busiest shopping districts in the Bronx and is always full of pedestrians. They began to record as soon as we walked out of the building as we headed towards Third Avenue and turned towards Willis Avenue. The filming was catching people's attention and many were beginning to stop and look. The interview was being conducted in Spanish in a community that was majority Puerto Rican/Latino, thus it was easy for the majority of the people to understand what was happening. The interviewers first asked me about myself, my background, and what I did for a living. Then they asked me about the dinner. They wanted me to explain why we invited Fidel to the Bronx and what my reaction was to the reception Fidel received. Fidel's visit to the Bronx was still on the minds of many people in the borough the day after our event. They all seemed to associate with my personal background, a Puerto Rican who had come straight from Puerto Rico as a child to the streets of the South Bronx, and was still living and working in the same neighborhood. I could see many people nodding in agreements with my answers about why we did what we did. I remember stating, "It was the correct thing to do regardless of our views on Fidel Castro or Cuba."

I remember emphasizing the fact that we believed that the mayor's actions of snubbing Fidel from the dinner that he had planned for all the United Nations heads of state was disrespectful. I remember that after I spoke a few folks began to clap and the camera crew turned to record that as well. They also interviewed one of the pedestrians who agreed with our decision to invite President Castro to the Bronx, and that he wished he had been able to attend.

The interview was over in about half an hour and we all returned to my office where they packed their equipment and left. I picked up where I had left off to finish what I had started in the early morning and to prepare to meet Franklin downtown for the early evening debate at NY 1 News.

# THE DEBATE

The debate at NY 1 was not as much a debate as I had thought it would be. I was glad because I really was not feeling up to debating a person who I respected, even if we had some differences.

Badillo had been part of the New York and Puerto Rican political landscapes since before I was introduced to any form of politics and was still in grade school. From the 1960s to the 1980s, there was no other popular Latino politician in New York and, for a time, even the United States, than Herman Badillo. For many of our parents, Badillo was like the Puerto Rican Jackie Robinson. He was considered a trailblazer who had come to New York from Puerto Rico as an orphan at the age of five, and went on to graduate from City College and the Brooklyn Law School at the top of his class. He was also a certified public accountant. He was the first to hold many political positions, including serving as the first Puerto Rican city agency commissioner, the first Puerto Rican borough president (The Bronx), and the first Puerto Rican elected to Congress. He should have been the first Puerto Rican mayor of New York City, but that is another story for another time. As a child growing up in New York, I remember how a struggling Puerto Rican community looked to Badillo as a symbol of hope and pride.

I respected Herman Badillo, but had several differences with him over the years, such as the time when he was commissioner of Housing Preservation and Development. In that role he headed the Department of Relocation and was responsible for a program dubbed, Operation Renewal (we called it, "Operation Removal"), which was a project to make way for the luxury buildings that exist in the West Side of Manhattan today.

The project caused the majority Puerto Rican community from the West Side of Manhattan that had been living there for decades to relocate under the false promise that many would be able to come back. Most never returned and wound up moving to the South Bronx. I also had a major difference with Badillo, who as a Democrat campaigned for Comptroller of New York City, on a "fusion" ticket with Republican Rudy Giuliani's mayoral campaign.

So here I was sitting opposite a Puerto Rican idol not knowing the exact rules of the debate. I was prepared to defend our actions in inviting President Fidel Castro to the Bronx, but I did not feel comfortable about going toe to toe on anything that deviated from that topic. To my relief, the procedure was not really a debate, but rather a chance for each of us to give our opinion on Fidel's visit to the Bronx.

I was clear and adamant on how we felt about the mayor's action of dis-inviting President Castro from the city's "welcoming" dinner for all of the world's delegates. I talked about why we found that that the mayor's action was disrespectful and why the Puerto Rican community in the Bronx decided to invite President Castro and welcome him to come and dine with us.

Mr. Badillo basically reiterated the Mayor's position for not inviting him to the dinner and other events held in the city. He spoke the same rhetoric that Mayor Giuliani and the members of the Cuban American Foundation were espousing every chance they had. He mentioned that the lack of political freedoms in Cuba and free elections in Cuba were reasons enough not to welcome him to our city. He sided with the Bronx Borough President, Fernando

Ferrer who also did not agree with our actions and did not welcome President Castro to the Bronx.

It was a cordial disagreement on both sides and the host did not cross-question either of us. It was short and to the point; two views were expressed without any bashing from either side. If anything it proved that two Puerto Ricans could have different opinions and not attack each other, as was the case in the numerous street protests that had taken place throughout the city. These protests were being promoted and organized by members of the Cuban exile community and funded by their organizations. Unlike our Bronx dinner, there was nothing indigenous about their anti-Fidel, anti-Cuba demonstrations. For the most part, the participants were all from out of state.

After the debate, Franklin and I commented on Badillo's position and wondered how such a powerful and respectable member of our Puerto Rican community had dwindled in stature to the point of becoming a spokesperson for a mayor who was tremendously out of touch with the minority communities of our city. We almost felt sad over how in the late stages of his career, he had become so out of touch with his own Puerto Rican community. I thanked Franklin for accompanying me and he wished me well on my trip to Puerto Rico the following day.

# FIRST FALLOUT FROM THE DINNER

I woke up the next day and was relieved that I had nothing on my schedule that had to do with the Fidel Castro dinner. I was still excited by what we had accomplished, but I was now looking forward to getting back to my personal life. I was so looking forward to going to Puerto Rico in the late afternoon. My family was also happy for me. Although it was a business trip, the fact that I was going to Puerto Rico and would visit my family and that was something they all knew I needed.

Right after breakfast I received a call from the station manager's secretary at WADO, the Spanish language radio station where I had a weekly radio program. The program was called, *"La Hora Del Taxista,"* (The Taxi Drivers Hour). She asked if I was available to meet with the station manager in the late morning and I said yes. I had requested to change our program's time slot and thought that the meeting was in reference to that request.

My program aired at midnight once a week and was dedicated to the growing and large Latino Gypsy and Livery cab industry. I provided some great music and vital information for many New York cabbies. During my undergraduate days I drove a gypsy cab for this developing industry. Yellow cabs refused to service the Bronx and that created the opening for anyone who had a car and wanted to make some money while providing a much-needed service to our community. It was illegal and dangerous, but it helped pay the bills. Thus, I always felt a kinship with the problems of this growing, but neglected industry. Gypsy cabbies were constantly abused by city agencies, the police, and unfortunately by criminals who found cabbies an easy mark for quick money.

I knew the industry quite well and convinced several sponsors, principally Gaseteria Gas Corporation, a Latino owned company, to sponsor me on a show exclusively for the cab industry. The president, Oscar Porcelli, loved the idea. He knew that many of his clients were cab drivers and felt that sponsoring the show would help increase those numbers and at the same time provide a service to that client base.

The program was an instant hit and everyone was quite happy with it. I was hoping that my request and our growing ratings was the reason for the meeting. When I arrived at the offices, I was not made to wait and was immediately brought into the station manager's office. He was cordial, but got straight to the point and told me that my show was being cancelled. I was shocked; I was not expecting this at all. Our program was quite popular, we always paid our program fees on time, and there was a lot of talk of expanding the show because the ratings were also good and growing for that late evening time slot.

I asked the station manager why? I persisted and asked why our program was being canceled when we were doing so well and there had never been any talk about any problems with our show? The station manager said that it was nothing personal. He told me that he liked me as well as the programming I had brought to the station. He said that it had nothing to do with anything I had done wrong, or with him. He told me that the decision came from above. I did not understand what he meant "from above" and asked him to clarify. He basically said that the owners and high-ranking executives decided all the programming and they no longer wanted my show to air on their station. At that moment I realized what was happening, even though I thought I would be immune from it: this was political fallout from the Fidel Castro dinner.

I asked him to be honest with me and tell me if my program was being cancelled because I was involved in the dinner for President Fidel Castro in the Bronx. He did not answer my question directly. He reiterated some mumbo jumbo about new programming, but was honest enough to say that perhaps me being so visible on the Fidel Castro visit to the Bronx did not help. I remembered then that radio station WADO, like other Spanish radio stations and Spanish TV networks had a heavy Cuban exile administration and answered my own question. I thanked him for being honest and for the support he gave when I first approached him with the idea of a program for the cab industry. I also thanked him for giving me the opportunity to be on the air and learn a little about the radio broadcasting industry. I got up, shook his hand, and left the office thinking how I had underestimated the reach of the Cuban exile community.

The program was not my main source of income. It was a side project, a part-time gig that I enjoyed doing once a week. The extra income I was generating from the program was good, but losing it was not going to really affect me financially. When I left the building I smiled, knowing that if that was the vindictive Cuban exiles best shot to get at me, it was a weak one. However, it did put me on high alert and I immediately brought in my family and closest friends and put everyone on notice. I was no longer naive to the fact that I now had some new enemies because of my involvement with the dinner for President Fidel Castro. This was nothing new for me. I had created enemies before because of my political beliefs and actions. Everyone in my family had experienced some degree of discomfort in the past due to my politics, and they learned to cope. They learned how to roll with the punches and absorb those discomforts, and as a result become stronger supporters of progressive causes and issues for social justice. In a way I was grateful that I had learned another lesson. I now knew that some members of the Cuban exile community had me on their radar, so I would not be caught off guard again.[xvi]

# ON THE PLANE AND WHAT A SURPRISE

I was so looking forward to leaving New York and being in Puerto Rico for that week. My business meetings would only take me a day or two and the rest of my time would be dedicated to a much-deserved short vacation with family and friends.

After going through the boarding process at Kennedy Airport I walked into the plane, found my seat and threw myself down with that "It's over, I'm home free attitude." For the first time since writing the press release, I was no longer preoccupied with anything that had to do with the dinner and President Fidel Castro's visit to the Bronx.

As I was waiting for the plane to taxi to the runway and take off I did everything possible to get myself into a totally relaxed mood. I was purposely thinking of my itinerary in Puerto Rico, seeing my parents who no matter what I was involved in would never inquire anything except my health and that of my family. Once the plane took off my mind was slowly relaxing more and more. Once the cabin crew made all the necessary safety announcements the televisions screens throughout the plane were automatically turned on and many of them, including mine were tuned into the CNN network. My eyes almost popped out of my sockets when to my surprise and shock, I saw CNN was re-broadcasting a segment of President Castro's visit to New York. The clip they used was that of President Fidel Castro receiving the oversized glove from my son. I could not hear what they were saying as I had not plugged in my headphones, but just the sight of seeing my son and Fidel on my screen and on so many other screens on the plane made me sink lower in my seat and hope that no one on the plane would see the similarity between the young boy standing next to Fidel Castro and myself.

I did not want anyone on that plane to approach me to ask anything about my son, the dinner, or me. I did not want to entertain any more conversations about the dinner. I was in escape mode and wanted to remain incognito. However, I realized that the dinner with President Fidel Castro in our South Bronx community had transcended our community and indeed was an event that had been seen around the world. I turned off the television screen and closed my eyes to try and catch up on some long awaited sleep.

# FINALLY IN PUERTO RICO - NO MORE TALK OF THE FIDEL DINNER, OR SO I THOUGHT!

I landed in Puerto Rico's West Coast Aguadilla airport in the early evening, got into my rental car and drove to the town of Mayagüez, where my meetings were to take place. I called my business associate in Mayagüez, José "Bebo" Avellanet. Bebo was very involved in all aspects of sports and was working in an administrative capacity with a basketball team of the Puerto Rican Basketball League. Bebo was also my contact person for Latino Sports on the island. He also had a radio program and had me on the air several times. Bebo knew about the dinner with President Fidel Castro and wanted to come. I had promised him a ticket if he was able to come to New York. Bebo had tried to work out his schedule to attend, but unfortunately was unable to do so.

When we spoke on the phone I advised him that I had landed and was on my way to Mayagüez. Bebo told me that there was a very competitive basketball game taking place at the Mayagüez Coliseum and encouraged me to meet him there. He told me that he would leave my name at the press gate. I had never been to the Mayagüez Coliseum for a basketball game and thought that watching a basketball game in Puerto Rico on my first night on the island would help me wind down and forget the last eight days of arduous work that felt more like eight months.

A basketball game in Mayagüez seemed to be the perfect way to leave New York behind and a perfect way to detox myself from the extreme stress generated by those days of non-stop strategizing, talking, working, and thinking about President Fidel Castro and his visit to the South Bronx. Mayagüez is a very sports-minded town and I knew that once I entered the coliseum I would be sitting with Bebo and his friends who were for the most part reporters, broadcasters, and basketball executives. I thought this would definitely help take my mind off the South Bronx and the dinner. I looked forward to the game and raced to get there by halftime.

When I arrived at the coliseum all the parking areas were packed. I remembered that basketball was really the national sport and had more fans attending than baseball. That is why Puerto Rico had, not one, but two professional basketball leagues at that time. They had the regular and older *Liga Superior* (the Superior League) and the newer *Liga Puertorriqueña* (The Puerto Rican League). Both leagues had basically the same players, but it gave the island almost year-round basketball. Puerto Rico's national basketball team had classified itself among the world's best, so games were usually packed to the limit.

It was difficult finding parking near the coliseum, but driving a small rental car has its advantages. One can take the risk of basically parking anywhere. After circling the coliseum once, I joined the several other illegally parked cars on a sidewalk and crossed over to the coliseum. I went to the press gate and as expected my credential was waiting for me. I entered the noisy, hot coliseum and it seemed like heaven to me. They were in the middle of a halftime show and the music and dancing was exactly what I needed. I was directed to the VIP and Press Area by one of the ushers and saw Bebo and many of his associates sitting around and having a good time drinking and analyzing the first half. Bebo came to greet me and sat me down next to him. He introduced me to some of his friends and excused himself. He told me he was going to get some beers for us. I didn't drink beer, or strong alcohol then or now, but drinking a cold native brewed *Medalla* beer in Puerto Rico is a ritual that I still practice to this day. When Bebo returned with the beers, he asked about the trip and before I answered, the half time was over and the announcer was prepping the crowd for the second half.

The announcer stated that before beginning the second half he wanted to take the opportunity to introduce a special guest who had just arrived from New York. That immediately got my attention as I was expecting a basketball player who perhaps was on my same flight, a last-minute addition to one of the teams? Perhaps someone I knew?

However, that was not what occurred. The announcer said: *Le queremos dar la bienvenida a Julio Pabón, el señor que organizó la cena para Fidel Castro en el Bronx* (We want to welcome Mr. Julio Pabón, the person who organized the dinner for Fidel Castro in the Bronx). I almost fell off my seat as the spotlight and attention turned toward me. I was confused and did not know how to react. It was just a few seconds, but it felt like forever. My mind was racing with thoughts of not knowing what was about to happen. Should I stand as Bebo and his friends were urging me to do? But I did not want to be a human target for any crazy half- drunk anti-Cuban, or anti-communist fan that would want to throw whatever they were holding at me.

I reluctantly stood up and to my incredible surprise the coliseum broke out in a loud and thunderous applause. I looked around and saw the people sitting immediately next to me, applauding with gusto as they shook their heads in agreement. It was as if I had done something to also make them feel proud of being Puerto Rican. At that moment I forgot the stress and the tension. I smiled, crossed my hands across my chest like an X, and thanked them. I was so relieved. It was as if weights had been lifted from my shoulders. I had felt the love and respect that I was being given by my people thousands of miles from the Bronx, but as I was taught many years earlier, Puerto Rico is home. I sat down, but could not concentrate on the game as people were personally congratulating me, patting me on the back and throughout the game offering to buy me a beer. Throughout that entire second half I kept thinking of how a press release turned into an invitation and that invitation turned into an event that I would never forget. An event that reached many corners of the country and other parts of the world that perhaps I would never know, but as I was experiencing that night in Mayagüez there were many people that agreed with our action. Like the night of the dinner when I was the last one to leave the restaurant and walked alone to my car feeling proud of what we had accomplished, I again was feeling proud next to thousands of people that validated the fact that we indeed scored a KNOCKOUT with Fidel's visit to the South Bronx. Indeed, we made history.

* * *

# STATEMENTS FROM THE THREE
# YOUTHS WHO GAVE FIDEL PRESENTS

I have tried to write my feelings, thoughts and experiences so that we can have a written account for all future generations. History was made that night on October 23, 1995 in the South Bronx. As my good friend and contributing writer to Latinosports.com, the late Howard Goldin told me when I had expressed doubts about continuing to write this manuscript: "Julio, one day Fidel, you, and everyone that was involved in that dinner will no longer be here. Everyone would have forgotten and there will be no written history of that historic event. Therefore, it is important that you write that experience."

I thanked Howard and the many other friends and family who gave me that push and words of encouragement that I needed. However, the words of the three young people—---Elena who was ten, Vanessa who was thirteen and Julio Antonio who was fifteen – inspired me the most, because when I listened to what they said, I realized that they represent the future. We really did this for them: our youth, represented by three young Latinos/as who helped to make history in the South Bronx in 1995, perhaps not even knowing the impact of their contribution. Therefore, I invited each to share their experience about that evening of October 23, 1995.

I believe it is important to include the perspective of the three youngsters who gave Fidel the gifts that evening, and who at that point in their lives were young enough to only experience the innocence of youth and not the politics of the times.

The following is their recollection of what they experienced that evening:

**Elena Flores:**
I was 10 years old when I met Fidel Castro. I was young, but I knew that people's views on him were sharply divided. My background in the political scene was pretty active for a 10-year old. With my mom and stepfather, I had been on bus rides to Washington, DC for protests and was present for similar rallies in NYC. We chanted his name in these rallies--in his favor. People chanted his name back--against him. Perhaps I couldn't fully appreciate what it was to meet Fidel, but I recognized that it was a big deal.

My memory is a little hazy on the play-by-play, but starting from the beginning, I remember my stepfather telling me that I would present Fidel with a bouquet of white roses. I asked why white roses instead of the usual red. As far as I knew, white flowers were given at someone's death in the United States. My stepfather explained that the white roses were symbolic of a famous poem written by Cuban intellectual and political leader José Martí. I don't remember whose idea it was, but I was going to ask him to autograph the evening's program for me after giving him the flowers.

We always spoke Spanish at home but it was more casual, and I was nervous about saying something more formal and eloquent when I offered the flowers and asked for the autograph. My mom helped me put together a few sentences that I practiced with her as we got ready and while we were at the venue.

I remember lining up next to the stage. When it was our turn and when I found myself actually standing next to him, I became overwhelmed by a combination of wanting to deliver the lines as practiced with my mom, how tall Fidel actually is, hearing and seeing all the cameras flashing. Fidel had kind eyes and seemed to genuinely appreciate the gesture of the flowers. I started to cry. I felt comfortable enough to get under his arm and cry some more! I almost forgot to get the autograph, but I luckily realized I had the program in my hand and still had a sentence to deliver. I handed him the program, which he signed. It was a successful exchange if I do say so myself.

**Vanessa Ramos:**
I was 13 years old. I remember my mother telling me that she was taking me to one of Julio's events. At first I thought it was one of his baseball MVP awards that he would have with famous baseball players.

I remember getting there and seeing a whole bunch of security, helicopters, barricades, police everywhere. I remember people protesting, on one side and others cheering on the other side. I remember, seeing people on rooftops and knowing that this must have been really important. The energy was really high.

I remember walking through all of that and I remember that I was told that Castro was going to be there.

I remember being met at the door by Julio who walked us in and the place was so packed it looked like a dance club on a Friday night. It was like shoulder-to-shoulder people. I mean it was really packed walking into the restaurant.

Julio briefed me and told me I was going to give Fidel Castro these Latino Sports hats. He told me to be calm and just go up on stage, give him the hats and shake his hand. "You shake his hand, you say hi," I believe he said. I said, O.K., but I was 13. So I did not know anything about Castro. All I knew was that he was the president of Cuba. I did not know how serious the whole moment was, what it actually meant.

So I remember going up on stage and seeing how packed it was, I mean it was a packed house. Flashes everywhere, all I saw was, flash, flash, and flash. It was then that I began to get nervous. But I remember Elena going first and giving him the flowers. I saw how it was being done, so I relaxed a little and said, OK I can do this. I saw Fidel with this big Kool-Aid smile on his face and thought he's cool and that made me feel more comfortable.

So now it's my turn and I go next to him, shake his hands, give him the hats, and he kisses me on the cheek. I remember feeling his beard. Everyone begins to clap and cheer. I still did not understand what just went down. It was not until a few years later when I was having a conversation with some of my friends and everyone started talking about all the famous people that they had met and I said, "Hey I also met someone famous." My friends said, "Yeah, whom did you meet?" I said I met Fidel Castro, the President of Cuba. They did not believe me, they said, "No you didn't." I remember laughing and said, "Yes, I met him in the Bronx." I then realized that happened when I was so young that a lot of people didn't even realize that Fidel Castro came to the Bronx. So I tell them the story how I met him at Jimmy's Bronx Café and how I shook his hands. They were all doubting me, saying, "yeah right." Thinking back I don't believe my age group really understands Cuba, or the whole situation about communism, socialism. I don't think even today a lot of people really understand the situation in Cuba.

But I do remember being there on that day and I remember feeling that I was part of something big. I just did not realize how big it really was until a few years later when I shared it with friends and no one believed me. I remember my mom telling me not to share that experience because she said that not everyone could understand and accept that type of information. She told me a lot of people might not like him. So don't go around telling everybody that you met Fidel Castro. I did not understand why she was telling me this, but I followed her advice and kept it to myself. However, I still said it here and there, bragging about it.

Today when I reflect back on that moment I think that you could go through your whole life without ever realizing how big the moments that you have been through really were. I feel today that I was part of history. Not just for the United States, but also for the Bronx, It was a bit of history for our borough. Now when I reflect I believe that Fidel Castro coming here to the Bronx, he helped to make the Bronx a little bit bigger than it was. When Julio asked me if I would have a problem sharing my experiences of that night meeting Fidel Castro I told him I would not. In fact I looked forward to being in his book because this way a lot of my friends won't think that I was bullshitting them.

### Julio Antonio Pabón (he was fifteen at the time)
That experience with Fidel was one of the first times I realized that narratives are based on experiences as well as pre-dispositions.

The day I met Fidel was very chaotic. Even though I'd traveled all the way to Cuba (illegally) I came face-to-face with the iconic leader right in my own backyard at Jimmy's Bronx Café. When I arrived, there were already hundreds of protesters outside, holding signs that read, "Fidel eats children" and *"Fidel Es Asesino"*. As I walked by, someone spit at me.

I was stationed with four secret service agents and a clipboard of the names of confirmed attendants. Under no circumstances was anybody getting in who was not on that list on my watch. I watched as secret service men removed people from the premises on my behest.

When I finally made it inside, my father took me backstage where Fidel was waiting. He was a tall, imposing figure and he stood out above the crowd. We snaked our way through the crowd and my father introduced me. I gave President Castro a firm handshake and he smiled, "*Mucho gusto, caballero.*" He had such soft hands. This man had been to jail multiple times and trekked through the jungles of Cuba fighting militants, yet his hands were soft and welcoming. He was not loud or militant.

I had never seen so many cameras in my life and though I'd never been nervous on a stage before, I was that moment. I remember handing him a welcoming gift, a big boxing glove that was a nod to his passion for the game and the Cuba's dominance in the sport. He cracked another smile, bigger and brighter. All I remember at that moment is the sound of a thousand cameras clicking. He put on the glove and raised his hand. Flashing lights blinded me as I looked into the roaring crowd. That photo of Fidel and I was famous in Cuba and infamous here.

I recently returned to Cuba and was eating in a *Paladar* (small family owned restaurant) with the owner and a few friends and I mentioned that I had met Fidel in the Bronx. He takes a long stare at me and asks me to follow him. We walk to the front of the restaurant and there is a TV with a photo slideshow. As the photos keep passing, he explains to me that he personally curated this slideshow of the most important photos of the last 55 years of the triumph of the revolution. In Spanish he says that he has access to hundreds of photos. They are of all the Cuban heroes. Fidel, Che, Camilo and Celia Sánchez. Then there are other photos of Fidel with Mandela, Malcolm X and Ted Turner. Finally, he pauses on my photo of Fidel with the boxing glove and takes a long stare at me. "*Esta foto es muy importante en este país. Es un honor tenerte en mi restaurante.*" (This photo is very important in this country. It's an honor to have you in my restaurant) One photo, two narratives.

# EPILOGUE

Twenty-one years later, looking back. I remember we went through a lot, but it was all worth it. The after effects of that dinner might not have given me any recognition, or brought me anything to put on my wall or lay on a shelf. It was the first time that I ever worked so hard and tirelessly on an event that was not part of any planned job assignment, community organization, or movement.

In fact, I had lost a lot in that event. I had expenses that never got reimbursed. I lost a major sponsor, a radio show, and never made a dollar from anything resulting in the organizing of that dinner. It caused me a lot of stress and loss of sleep organizing such a major event in such little time.

It also cost me an easy revenue stream, as my Spanish radio program had been generating some extra income for me. However, it did reward me in many other ways. It brought me closer to some members of my family. My then - wife, Liz Figueroa, gave me the space, support, and guidance that I needed. I involved my eldest daughter Kimberly in this event without really discussing it with her. Her workload doubled for those few days that were like weeks. I threw things at her without notice and she handled everything like a trooper. Our bond grew stronger after the event. I was proud of my son, Julio

Antonio who stepped up to the plate at a very young age when I most needed him to. He not only handled the main door when we had no one else, but also accepted the role of giving Fidel the glove. That simple action marked him in many ways and perhaps brought unnecessary attention to a fifteen-year-old, attention that may have affected him in some ways, even today. He too has been a target of government harassment, but to our pride he has handled those episodes well and has continued in his own progressive path. My daughter Taína, though not involved in the planning of the dinner and who was living away from home, made the time to come and support the event against the criticism of her boyfriend's mother, a Cuban exile who had nothing nice to say about Fidel and insisted he would not show up. Thus all my three children were part of that historic moment. Once again I was reminded that I am blessed to have a family that comes together to support each other when needed. All my children, Kimberly, Taína and Julio Antonio were tested in battle and just like rookie soldiers who survive a war and come back stronger, so did my children become better prepared for what life has to offer. I am proud of all my children who supported and helped make that dinner the success that it was.

Looking back, I realized how much that dinner taught me about myself, my family, and other important things in my life.

I am forever proud of what we did. My heart and soul has been stamped with the pride of the son of a poor Puerto Rican migrant farm worker who taught me the value of standing up against any injustice no matter what the consequences might be.

＊　＊　＊

# ACKNOWLEDGEMENTS

I am grateful to everyone that participated in making that idea of writing a simple news release into the historic event that it has become. Thank you to all of the more than three hundred guests that braved the circumstances of the times and came to the dinner with President Castro. Although many came out to protest against a mayor's insult to another fellow Latino rather than in support of a leftist, or a socialist leader they did not understand. The fact is that in the end they all helped to make history in the Bronx with overwhelming support. I give special thanks to David Galarza who was the one that implanted the idea in my mind, even though I might have cursed him out during those stressful three days of organizing the gargantuan event.

Carlos Nazario who as then president of the young and developing National Puerto Rican Business Council (NPRBC) had both faith and courage in what at first seemed like a crazy idea by having the organization serve as the main sponsor of the dinner. I am forever thankful to him for trusting my judgment.

Without having a restaurant to list on our news release it would not have had the professional aspect it needed to show that we were seriously taking on the mayor. Thank you Jimmy Rodríguez who at first did not understand what he was signing on to do and all the political ramifications of my request. However, he still trusted my judgment as good friends usually do. However, I am sure that at one point he might have wanted to do more than curse me when his restaurant was briefly closed by the Secret Service preparing for Fidel's visit.

I want to thank Congressman José Serrano for first warning me about the possible repercussions of our idea for a news release, but trusting the crazy idea and adding his name as a supporter. His backing and his call to the head of the U.S. Cuban Interest Section, Fernando Remírez in Washington helped put additional attention on a news release that turned into an official invitation to President Fidel Castro.

Thank you Jerry "Fast Feet" Fontanez for saying, "I got you," when I asked for his help with security and taking on the assignment like a professional with the five other black belts that he recruited for this assignment.

To my friends, Franklin Flores and Mickey Melendez, for stepping up to the plate to help organize the logistics of the dinner, a dinner that would have taken anyone else weeks, perhaps months to organize, but that we were able to do in less than three days.

A special thank you to my family Liz Figueroa my wife at the time, my daughter Kimberly and my son, Julio Antonio. Thank you Liz for giving me the space and support to do what I needed to do during that crazy and stressful period and for being the best partner to have a son with. My son, Julio Antonio, who at the young age of 15 made a personal decision to stand up for positive values by volunteering to help with the dinner and be one of the three youths to personally greet Fidel and give him gifts. My daughter Kimberly who was caught in the middle of something she had not planned for or expected, while working with me for our other businesses. When the immense workload increased in the office due to the unplanned event, she came through like a seasoned professional managing my other businesses by herself and helping with the increased workload in the office.

Without any of these individuals the dinner with Fidel Castro would have never been as successful as it was. Our combined efforts demonstrated that the will and tenacity of the Puerto Rican community in New York City to stand up for positive values and justice was still very much alive in 1995. Our forefathers who paved the way for everything that all Latinos can enjoy today would be proud of what a few individuals with no resources and despite many naysayers can accomplish when they combine their resources.

I also must thank the following individual who once I decided to embark on this project came into my life and supported me in many ways to finally get this final manuscript ready for publication.

Friends and family had been encouraging me for years to write some of my personal experiences growing up in the South Bronx. I have been a public speaker at conferences, colleges and other events where I have been asked or contracted to speak and almost always someone would come up to me and ask, whether I had considered writing a book.

After hearing this so often, I finally gave the idea of writing a book serious thought. I began a novel dedicated to my mother's life that I started years ago, after her passing. For many reasons I had stopped and had not been able to build up the focus and energy to continue.

In 2014, as a result of some major changes in my professional life, I found myself with more time on my hands, and again thought about perhaps finishing the novel I started writing on my mother. However, my son Julio Antonio, and my other spiritually adopted Godson, Dario Lopez Jr. kept talking to me about seriously sitting down and writing something now during this new period in my life.

Both concluded that something shorter (or so it seemed) like the story of Fidel's visit to the South Bronx was the perfect piece. I thought a lot about it, spoke to a few people and decided that perhaps that was a good idea. Dario went further and began to explain the entire publishing scenario that had preoccupied me. He visually demonstrated the process of doing self-publishing and a digital book. That was it. I was convinced about the story and the plan to publish a book.

However, like the dinner in 1995, this was not something I could do by myself. Many people played a role that contributed to my accomplishment of writing this book and I want to list them all.

Thank you Julio Antonio and Dario. Thank you, Liz Figueroa who for so many years had encouraged me to write, even to the point of telling me to record my thoughts and that she would transcribe them. Thank you for the encouragement when I first started thinking of doing this book.

Thanks to my wife, Blanca Canino-Vigo, who looked out for my health while putting up with my crazy schedule and other projects (like running for office) while allowing me the space to sometimes seclude myself and miss out on the many outdoor fun activities and family events that make our relationship special.

Thanks to the entire staff at the Centro Library and Archives/Hunter College. Your support in helping a guy who had not done any academic research in over 25 years and to help me feel comfortable and find much of what I was looking for was very helpful.

Thanks to the staff of the 42nd St Public Library periodicals section where I spent many hours and days reading every New York newspaper for the period covering October 1995.

Thank you Daniel Acosta Elkan, a guest in Mi Casa Tu Casa Guesthouse who saw me struggling with periodicals and volunteered to help me with The New York Times of October 1995.

Thank you David Galarza, Carlos Nazario, Franklin Flores, Mickey Melendez, Kimberly Pabón, Jerry Fontanez, Liz Figueroa, Jimmy Rodríguez, former Cuban Minister Fernando Remírez, and Cuban Minister of Foreign Affairs Bruno Rodríguez for giving me the time to interview you and help refresh my memory on what we did in 1995.

Thank you to the late, Howard Goldin, one of our senior writers for Latinosports.com for your words of wisdom. When I was going through one of those periods of not wanting to continue writing and doubting the value of writing this experience you encouraged me by saying: "You need to write this story so that it will be forever remembered." Your words resonated and gave me the lift I needed at that time.

Thank you to the folks in Cuba. Thank you José Berrios from the Puerto Rican Mission in Cuba and his wife, Daisy who loved the project and together were my guides throughout many of my visits to Cuba. Thank you for introducing me to Roberto Chile, Fidel's personal photographer for many years and who provided me with many pictures and video of Fidel's visit to the Bronx and for suggesting the perfect name for the book, "Knockout."

Thank you Silvia Johoy for your persistent nudging and arranging a meeting with Eugenio Suárez Pérez, Director of the Office of Historical Affairs – Council of the State who upon meeting loved the project and supplied me with additional photos and footage that helped me tremendously. Thank you Eugenio.

Special thanks, to my dear friend and translator, Lizette Colón, for taking on the difficult task of translating President Castro's speech from Spanish to English. No easy task, but you, 93-year-old Jerry Weissman and your daughter, Gloriela Iguina-Colón took on the job and helped provide us with the first English draft.

Thank you Wally Edgecombe who saw me struggling trying to find an editor and recommended Ronnie Lovier. Ronnie, thank you for taking on this project at the last minute and working tirelessly to help me meet my own personal deadline. I could not have found a better editor, and one who would also comprehend my political thinking. Also a truly heartfelt *"Gracias"* to Wally who worked on the last and final translation of Presidents Castro's speech that needed that special editing that only a Cuban who had lived in Cuba before the revolution and who was present that night at the dinner could give.

Thank you to Robert Carillo, Liz Figueroa and Nelson Dennis who volunteered to be my first focus group to read the original first edited draft. Your comments and suggestions were very helpful. Special thanks to Gabriel "Gabe" Devries who took on the task to be the final editor to read through the manuscript and give it that last edit required.

Special thanks to Dr. Ricardo Fernández, President of Lehman College who agreed to write the forward. There was no greater pleasure for me than to have the forward written by the president of the college that I graduated from in 1975 and who also attended that historic dinner. Thank you Dr. Fernández.

The universe conspired to put me in contact with all the people that worked with me during that period in 1995 and with all the people that came into my life during the writing, research and editing. Now, twenty-one years later from that historic event I am eternally grateful to all of them.

Message To Our Youth

There are many lessons learned from that historic dinner with President Fidel Castro in the South Bronx. One in particular that I want to emphasize to the youth of today who are living in a fast and engulfing social media world that allows us to connect with more people than ever before, it also distances us from the very people with whom we need to be in greater contact. If you can get one lesson from what we all did in those nine days in October of 1995 with very little technology is that nothing is impossible and nothing is stronger than the love that you give when working, or organizing for something that is culturally, or politically correct no matter what the odds.

I believe that there are many more issues today and in the future that will need a few more "*atrevidos*."

$$* \quad * \quad *$$

# FIDEL'S SPEECH (TRANSLATED FROM ORIGINAL SPANISH TEXT)

SPEECH BY COMMANDER IN CHIEF FIDEL CASTRO RUZ, FIRST SECRETARY OF THE CENTRAL COMMITTEE OF THE COMMUNIST PARTY OF CUBA AND PRESIDENT OF THE COUNCILS OF STATE AND MINISTERS TO A REPRESENTATION OF PUERTO RICAN BUSINESSMEN, IN THE BOROUGH OF THE BRONX, NEW YORK, ON OCTOBER 23, 1995, "YEAR OF THE CENTENARY OF THE FALL OF JOSE MARTI".

(Shorthand version - COUNCIL OF STATE)

Dear friends and distinguished daring ones:

If you see me having a little trouble seeing. Please bear in mind that these are the necessities of modern times and of electronics and those light bulbs are intense.

Julio said, "I think that they would have required the stadium—the baseball one, right?" (laughter) - but it seems to me that I am looking at a stadium in this magnificent "room" in Jimmy's restaurant (laughter, applause), who has been so bold and brave as to lend it to us tonight.

In all honesty, I have been impressed by the words of Julio Pabón and José Serrano. I have very much liked the simple, direct, clear, frank way in which they speak; also they know what they are saying, and say a lot, and they say it with all the necessary care.

As they talked about the things that unite us and bring us closer to the great Latin American or Hispanic American family, I remembered, among other things, the language that unites us, which is able to express many feelings like those expressed here, and that it is able to arouse such emotions like those that my colleagues of the Cuban delegation and I have felt here tonight (applause)

I believe that before I continue, I must clarify this serious problem in the Major Leagues, because I see that you are Cleveland fans (laughter), and I, who have been interviewed quite often on television, almost all reporters spoke about this matter.

There is something strange, and that is that what most Americans know about me is that I like baseball (laughter and applause). Sure, I like many other sports, but every American who visits us brings me a ball or a glove or a bat (laughter), or a book with the biography of a big baseball star, or the biography of many players and their records, the championships, everything; but they identify me—and that's good—as an athlete and as a baseball player.

Today they gave me another bat and a ball, and with all of the ones I have received, I can definitely start a museum (laughter).

On television I was asked, "Well, what team do you support?" You can't do that (laughs). I was just coming from Uruguay, de Bariloche, from a summit of state and government leaders from Latin America, and I had no time to read, not even a cable, or a newspaper; it was all speeches and more speeches—at least with mine, I am occupied while others get bored (laughter and applause).

Now, as you know, I am considered the Olympic winner when it comes to delivering the shortest speeches, when it comes to a summit and when they limit them to no more than five or six minutes. In Bariloche I gave one that lasted three and a half minutes, and that was a record breaker (laughter); seven minutes in Cartagena, six minutes at the summit meeting of chiefs of state at the United Nations, and that was because I read a little slower so I could emphasize a few things.

So that in many interviews, they asked me that question and I was amazed. If I had known that here in the Bronx you were rooting for Cleveland (laughter), then I would have to say, "Look, don't get me into trouble " (laughter). I remembered that as a friend of Ted Turner, I would have to say: "Well, as I am a friend of Ted Turner, I have to say I root for the Braves."

Today I was asked again and I said: "You're going to get me into trouble with half of the country, not for political reasons but for sporting reasons" (laughter). Well, I already made my choice, although I am not entirely affiliated with it, I have to keep in mind what someone told me: "Hey, the fact is that there was a player from Cleveland who hit two home runs and also took out who knows who on first base; he was a hero and I think that the man was Puerto Rican". So having said that, I hope you will be understanding and forgive me for that (laughter and applause).

They were talking to me about a good Cuban athlete, and they wanted him to come here to play. Well, everything is possible right? We must have to get I don't know how many permits (laughter), but with our good will would never be lacking in that case.

I insist once again that I liked the clarity and the courage with which we have spoken tonight, and also the wisdom, which is the same that I have to use here.

But there is a criticism, because one of them said that here there are progressive people and there are business people and I say: Since when can you be sure that business people are not progressive? (Laughter and applause.) Why? Because we don't have to make that distinction, as all have contributed, all are here, all have honored us greatly, they have all given us infinite encouragement, all of them have taught us, all of them have educated us and, above all, they have widened the circle of our great Latin American family, our great human family; when we have been told that tonight many more wanted to come, that in the Bronx there are more than almost half a million Puerto Ricans, I was astonished (applause).

I was surprised to know that there are not only Puerto Ricans, but also that there are Dominicans, Cubans and from other nationalities, Uruguayans— we were just told (laughter)– that there were also Americans from North America, Panamanians, and from everywhere. It is an unforgettable lesson for us that we were not able to understand that important human dimension, to understand that there are so many brothers and sisters among you (applause).

There were conversations about the Cuban emigration and about Miami, New Jersey—yes it was mentioned (laughter)—but we cannot even think, and I think one of them put it clear that most Cubans living in the United States are in favor of the blockade, because we know of many, many, many who are not and cannot be in favor of the blockade for many reasons, among others, the ones so brilliantly presented here tonight.

The United States was traditionally the land for the Cuban migration in past centuries, and even many Cubans came to fight for the independence of the United States—almost nobody remembers that. In the days of Washington, in the difficult days of a grueling war, they came from Cuba and fought. Spaniards also came to fight for the independence of the United States; we could say that they came over the centuries.

There were times when our country had a divided opinion, because we were the last ones to become independent from Spain, and had more than 300,000 slaves; indeed, the Spaniards were masters of the administration, the army, trade, and Cubans owned land and slaves. Among many of them an annexationist sentiment prevailed because they were afraid that what happened in Haiti could occur in Cuba, and of what led to the Haitian revolution, which was the first country to become independent.

Some Cubans thought at that time that the only way to save our country was to join the American nation, and within the United States there were currents favoring the annexation as they believed they were going to gain two votes in the Senate, in a time when the issue of slavery was discussed even more than the Helms-Burton Act (cheers), whether slavery was going to be abolished or not.

Do not forget that even though this great country, which was the forerunner of modern revolutions, as it even preceded the French Revolution—though with ideas that came mainly from Europe, and fought for years for its independence and declared itself independent—said, that it considered that there were self-evident truths that all men are born free and equal and that the Creator gave them certain rights. In reality, among these rights and these self-evident truths granted by the Creator, none were intended for slaves, and it was only after almost 80 years of hard struggle and civil war, that the slaves were emancipated. But there were Cubans who favored annexation, others strongly opposed it, and that was a great struggle.

After our wars of independence many Cubans sought refuge in the United States. They were organized here, they worked here; the best known, the most prestigious one, was the greatest national hero, José Martí (applause).

During the republic, many Cubans came to the United States looking for jobs, not in the early years, but rather when some momentum had already been reached in the sugar industry, the population grew and employment decreased. Here in New York, New Jersey, Miami, Cubans lived in many places before the revolution and we met with them and they supported us—some of them returned to Cuba but others are still living in America, and during these days had the pleasure of greeting a few of them... It was really the Revolution that opened the doors to emigration to the United States. The first who emigrated after the Revolution were, of course, those people linked to the Batista regime who had committed many crimes—it is estimated that about 20,000 people were killed—and hundreds of criminals and thieves took refuge in the United States; it was an emigration of a political nature.

When the first revolutionary laws were applied, a range of interests were affected because there can be no revolution and there has not been anywhere, not even in America during the revolution of independence, without affecting many interests. I can imagine how many English were affected by the independence of the United States and would leave for England; then there were wars between the United States and England. The Revolution also affected interests and a part came here; but the great reality is that the vast majority of those who came after did so for economic reasons, since we were in the vicinity of a country that enjoyed twenty times more income than us, much higher wages.

The phenomenon of migration is universal, just that in the case of Cuba it was argued that all who could come should come. That privilege was not granted to anyone. In Puerto Rico for its special political status (Puerto Ricans) did have the right to travel, to come and go; Cubans and other Latin Americans did not.

Today one of the biggest problems in the world and one of the greatest fears of developed countries is immigration. You see how Resolution 187 in California took hold, how some people talk of putting a larger wall than the Berlin wall on the border of Mexico and the United States (laughter), and there are those who advocate building three walls.

Cubans were told: "Come, you will be well received." At first we lost doctors, then we lost teachers, we lost everything: skilled workers, executives, directors. They were more likely to come to this country. Laws that gave the Cubans the rights that did not exist for any other citizen of Latin America and the world, and it was logical that a mass migration should occur.

But we were the ones who opened the doors, the Revolution opened the doors to this emigration (applause), and our policy is: anyone who wishes to emigrate is free to do so. And they came in waves, until the US imposed measures and restrictions. That is why the Cuban emigration grew in all those places.

To be sure, they were well received, they were granted immediate residency, de facto, financial assistance, jobs and facilities that others did not. Did you need a passport? No. You could come on a boat…on a hijacked plane or in a raft (laughter), and you were asked: "Sir, who are you? What passport do you have? And you would answer: "I am an anti-socialist, I do not agree with the political problems of Cuba…"

Actually, in those early years, there was very strong differentiation among those who came. We ourselves did not have sufficient understanding that many of those émigrés were economic migrants…and we saw them as enemies of the Revolution.

Of course, some of those compatriots were used for subversive activities against Cuba, to organize expeditions to destroy the Revolution, and so we had many problems and serious difficulties; we had the Bay of Pigs invasion. We took thirteen hundred prisoners and, as we have said before, there was not one who received a blow or even a rifle butt because of those principles that we maintained throughout our Revolutionary struggle.

I can assure you here, categorically, that those are principles that we have never abandoned (applause), and never in our country have we threatened the physical integrity of persons. That's one of the things against which we fight, against those who have tortured thousands of our comrades. And I can assure you more: I have read something about revolutions and I have read about history, and I think the most generous revolution that has ever existed is the Cuban revolution (shouts and applause). I say this quite frankly.

You can ask any of those who came from Girón if anyone yanked their hair (laughter), despite the heat of combat and although they had killed or wounded hundreds of our comrades. Those are the principles of the Revolution, because a lie, slander, infamy repeated once, a thousand times, a million times, can never become true! (applause). It doesn't matter how many people believe a lie, a lie cannot ever be transformed into the truth.

We lived in times of the Cold War, perilous times, we lived these dangers, suffered the blockade from the first moments, difficult moments, and we did not have the organization or the experience we have today. Friends and allies emerged assisting us when oil supplies, machinery, parts, were all suspended. We receive outside help for which we were always…grateful, no matter what happened later.

We had to go through a very difficult stage, but Cubans—as you know—are very ingenious. If you go to Havana you will see many cars from 1940, 1950, 1960; that is not like New York, where what you see are all new cars and almost all are Japanese (laughter, applause)… It is true that they have a Soviet engine consuming so much gasoline they need a refinery in the rear (laughter), or parts that Cubans built, that made them work…these cars are now worth more than a new car. Do you know why? Because they are museum pieces (laughter), and museum pieces are always more expensive.

We went through very difficult times. All our machinery was American, in transportation, factories and tractors. All that changed, and in that bitter struggle, we experienced pirate attacks, invasions, and assassination attempts galore.

I can assure you that against us so many assassination plans were drawn up, that I could give one to each of those present here (laughter). I do not want to do that, but that explains the little miracle that I am talking to you, because, according to the calculation of the odds, I should be in the afterlife, but I assure you it would not be in hell (laughter and applause)… I will not discuss beliefs in purgatory because we have already gone through a long purgatory (applause and shouts of "In Heaven"). In heaven, surely; but we have not searched for a place in heaven for us. Yes, I can tell you that we have wanted to find a place in heaven for our people (applause). That has been our struggle.

Perhaps with the experience of today, the realities of today and what we have learned today, we should have made a clearer distinction between those who emigrated for political reasons and those who emigrated for economic reasons. I can tell you even now that many who emigrated for political reasons today have excellent relations with the Revolution. That is, times change, life changes, and I can assure you that many of those Cubans are changing and that may constitute, if they do not already constitute, a silent majority who do not have the resources of others, the media access others have to lobby. They are specialized in lobbying, and that is why the battles confronting Serrano and other representatives in the House and Senate are so difficult, struggling against those measures that are truly cruel.

When I spoke at the United Nations yesterday, I said the blockade that kills men, women and children, young and old, was like silent atomic bombs.

None of you needs to repent for what you have done. Serrano or Julio spoke of history—because the two spoke, one after the other (laughter)—and, really, you are making history; you are making more than just history, you are being heroic (applause), because under certain conditions, the bravery of inviting the Cuban delegation, the courage to challenge prejudices, lies, slander, publicity; threats like those that have been mentioned, of not giving work to someone because he had a different attitude, are acts of aggression, are acts of pressure, are acts which strike the elementary principles of this country where you have been received and where you live.

And believe me, dear friends, the organized mafia that seeks to promote measures of the blockade against our country does not respect anyone at all, and I know of major political figures and businessmen who have been threatened, who have been intimidated with threats by the campaigns organized by the groups to defend through fascist methods their objectives and plans.

I know people in Miami who have to live underground. I know people in Miami who when they tell what happened, you almost cannot believe it… harassment at work, pursuing them at the club where they exercise and do other things, pursuing them in their homes, making threats by telephone, and above all, a psychological terror by radio and television, attacks, slanders.

In addition, they have taken families that have been traveling in a car with their children and the car had been shaken on the street as revenge, or because they have gone to a meeting in Havana, or because they are contrary to hostile measures such as the blockade. They have threatened the children, and I wonder if those are democratic methods, if they are humane methods, or are they methods that deserve to really be called what they are, fascist methods (applause), and have been used against …other countrymen. These methods must fail sooner or later.

We observe changes of opinion in the United States itself, and in a growing number of people and eminent personalities from the world of publicity, the press, the business world, who are already weary and tired of a senseless policy. As I have said: Is Cuba today the only country, and why? The only country that has not been at war with the United States, which has had historical relations, why is it the only country that is blockaded?

We have mentioned China, we have mentioned Vietnam, we have mentioned Korea. Soldiers from the United States and soldiers from those countries confronted each other in great battles. That has never occurred in relation to Cuba.

Blockade measures were not carried out against governments that disappeared more than 100,000 people. I said last night at a meeting in Harlem how, as a result of the invasion against Arbenz, governments of force were established in which there was no category of prisoners because all were totally disappeared and that is how more than 100,000 people disappeared since the fall of Arbenz. How right we are to defend ourselves!

What would the future of our country be if people utilizing those methods and those procedures would take over our country and that within 50 years our people would be mourning tens of thousands of missing persons? And that was not the only country; there are a few countries in Latin America where there were thousands of missing and murdered people.

I can say here with a morality as high as the Himalayas, that in our country we have never had death squads, nobody has ever gone missing, or ever been assassinated (applause). That is a truth that no one can deny as there are 11 million Cubans who have witnessed it; even those who are our adversaries will not say that, they could complain about other things, they want other things, they might not think the same way we do —and that is not, of course, the majority—but never could any of them claim that any of these things have occurred.

We are against the blockade of any country. For as it was said here, to whom is the blockade directed, who is affected? The people. Would it be fair to say: We do not like the Cuban Revolution and we will drop 10 nuclear bombs? That it is prohibited to sell to our country an aspirin, a single aspirin! For a headache, I will not say an Alka-Seltzer to help digestion? (laughter). That it is prohibited to sell cytostatic, medical equipment, a drug that can save lives? And I know cases of compatriots who have died because they could not secure the supplies in time, going around the world searching for medications that they are prohibited from selling us.

Regarding Cuba, there is not only an embargo, embargo is a weak word. We say a blockade, but what has been directed at Cuba is really an economic war, a political war.

The USSR no longer exists, and there is no socialist camp that attracted a great deal of publicity, propaganda attacks... Relations with China are excellent, with Vietnam, with everyone, and we are now all alone, and all the publicity artillery and hostility that was leveled at the whole socialist camp, is now directed at Cuba.

Yesterday we explained in Harlem what Cuba has done; I do not want to repeat myself. I will not be long-winded, but I have examples of how our country has sent more than 15,000 doctors to provide free services in the Third World—I don't think any other country has done that (applause): teachers, construction workers, scientists, researchers, agronomists by the tens of thousands.

Nicaragua asked us to send 2,000 teachers…to teach in the mountains, in the most remote areas to where you had to walk three days or ride a mule; and people lived there with very poor families in one room: the father, mother, seven or eight children, horse and a Cuban male of female teacher, because most were women (applause).

Remember how our country made 100,000 blood donations when the earthquake occurred in Peru. In ten days, 100,000 blood donations or 50,000 when the earthquake hit in Armenia or Iran, another country where there have been disasters, and aid to many countries in Latin America, even though we might no have had diplomatic relations with them. Those are the feelings, the social consciousness that the Revolution has taught our people; that has been the sense of humanity (and) solidarity with which we have worked.

With regard to Chernobyl, that great tragedy, I want you to know that in our country 13,000 children were treated for free. Cuba alone has assisted more children from Chernobyl than all the other countries in the world combined (applause). That has been our policy, our ethic.

I also mentioned something else, that we have shed our blood to help the African colonies obtain their independence (applause); we have fought against racists and fascists of South Africa apartheid; we have contributed decisively to the independence of Namibia; we have contributed decisively in the common struggle in collaboration with Angolans, Namibians, South Africans and Cubans, to bring about the demise of apartheid. Is it fair to blockade our country? Is it fair that a sick man should not be able to get a medication? (shouts of "No!") That a child should go without milk? (shouts of "No!") That the elderly be denied sustenance? (shouts of "No!") Well, we have had to endure the blockade that today is not justified, as it has become a matter of internal politics: those make a lot of noise in one state or another, and they believe that their votes will be decisive in elections. Unfortunately this is a factor that has had great impact.

What you do, what you promote is precisely the antidote to all that (applause). You are part of this great nation, you participate with tens of millions of men and women who speak the same language as us, men and women who speak Spanish, who have the same culture with the same pride in their countries of origin, as do others, for example the Irish people in their origins, in their history. You are a great force, and in a country where every group organizes to defend its interests, it's amazing the strength that you can build to the extent that you unite and are able to disseminate awareness of these problems.

It is sad that you have to fight, you have to perform the feat of confronting people not acting on feelings, not acting for ideals; those who fight with so much hatred, so viciously, who mount many campaigns against Serrano or Nydia, or many of the growing number who…have opposed the blockade and who have analyzed it from an ethical point of view, from a human point of view, from a standpoint of principle.

Our country has truly had to live in very trying situations. While we had the blockade, we traded with the socialist camp; after the socialist camp collapsed, we lost 75 percent of our imports and almost one hundred percent of our market. And yet, we have resisted. Why? Because of that consciousness that I referred to (applause), because of that sense of dignity, because of that sense of liberty, for that sense of solidarity, because what we have is not much but we share it among all, and no one was left out on the street, no one was left homeless; there were no shock policies, not one school, not one nursery was closed, not a single nursing home, not one clinic was closed.

In our country, every year there are not any fewer doctors, not any fewer teachers and professors but more teachers and professors; and we have thus reached the highest number of doctors per capita in the world, in all developed countries (applause), and the highest per capita of professors and teachers in the world; tens of thousands of scientists.

How would we have been able to achieve this? There has been talk of miracles, but I can assure you that your Cuban brethren have been capable of such a feat, achieved not by force but…because in our country it is the people who defend the Revolution, it is the people who are armed (applause). It would have been absolutely impossible to resist, and we not only resist, but are also beginning to raise our heads.

I'm sure your voices — because the press has kindly reported them—will be heard by our people and will be a huge injection of encouragement and stimulus, and that they will hear the words of Julio and Serrano, and appreciate the tenor and spirit of this event for which I express gratitude on behalf of the Cuban people.

But do not regret the heroism, never regret the justice, never regret the courage and daring because it has been the brave, firm people, the daring ones who have achieved the most beautiful things in history.

Always, regardless of philosophy, I give the example of Christianity for which it struggled, from those twelve apostles who began to spread around the world the doctrines of love and justice, to the thousands or who knows how many countless men and women who died defending their faith. If today Christianity exists, it is because there have been Christians who knew how to die on the cross, it is because there have been Christians who knew how to be devoured by lions rather than give up their ideals.

Those who insult or threaten you are not as fierce as those lions, nor are they so powerful, nor do they posses a higher intellect. Nor will you be weaker after this event; I am sure, absolutely sure, that you will be stronger. So we should truly be proud, you and us. We, for being the recipients of the honors and encouragement that men and women as excellent as you have bestowed upon us. And you because you make it possible for good causes to succeed, because you are just, courageous, noble, because you are generous and caring.

Thank you very much (prolonged applause).

The winner between President Fidel Castro & Mayor Giuliani
for the positive attention while in our city was,

Fidel Castro by a KNOCKOUT.

\*   \*   \*

# REFERENCES

i    Bureau of vital statistic. NYC DOHMH. 2000 Census. Department of City Planning

ii   Bureau of vital statistic. NYC DOHMH. 2000 Census. Department of City Planning

iii  It turned out that this was the largest gathering in the history of the United Nations as reported by the NY Times October 19th, 1995: Planning Pomp & Security for the U.N.'s Anniversary, page B 1.

iv  In 1989 the Baseball Writers Association of America (BBWAA) overlooked the rising Puerto Rican rising star, Ruben Sierra for the American League Most Valuable Player award. My reaction was to organize an event for Sierra that was to take place when the Texas Rangers visited New York in April of that year. The event took place at Yankee stadium. However, we wanted to do a community reception and I was introduced to Jimmy's father who owned, Marisco Del Caribe, a whole in the wall seafood restaurant under the Cross Bronx Expressway and Webster Ave. Mr. Rodríguez told me to speak to his son, Jimmy who loved the idea and we had our reception. After that first event, Jimmy and I developed a good relationship and we continued to give the awards every year at Jimmy's Bronx Café. The award, LatinoMVP is still given today and has become the oldest and most prestigious award given to a Latino baseball player.

v   I had known of the attempts on President Castro's life as they were widely reported in 1975, when the U.S. Senate convened the *Senate Select Committee to Study Governmental Operations with Respect to Intelligence Activities*. It was chaired by, Senator Frank Church (D-Idaho). The Church Committee stated that it substantiated eight attempts by the CIA to assassinate Fidel Castro in 1960-1965. However, during my research in Cuba I learned that the number of attempts on President Castro's life was much higher. Upon further research I learned that according to a retired chief of Cuba's counterintelligence, responsible for protecting Fidel Castro, Mr. Fabian Escalante estimated the number of assassination schemes or actual attempts by the CIA to be 638. Some of them were part of the covert CIA program dubbed *Operation Mongoose* aimed at toppling the Cuban government.

vi  Jimmy was referring to a Major League Baseball memo that went out to the players warning them not to visit Jimmy's Bronx Cafe because it was a place "frequented by unsavory characters." NY Daily News. Wednesday, August 23, 1995, "State Is Probing Slugger's Bx. Café" by Zachary Margulis, Juan González.

vii  Now that office is the Cuban Embassy in the United States.

viii  When David and I finished writing the press release I also had called out to my friend, Franklin Flores and sent him a copy. Franklin had a good working relationship with the Cuban Mission due to him and his Cuban wife, Nancy's work with Casa De Las Americas a New York based organization of Cuban emigrants who support the revolution. As a courtesy I asked Franklin to share the press release with his contacts at the Cuban Mission.

ix  When I interviewed the former head of the Cuban Interest Section in Washington, Fernando Remírez in Cuba. He too agreed that the dinner in the Bronx was quite historic in many ways and that it left a very positive impression on President Castro and all of the members of the Cuban delegation that attended.

x  The U.N. 50th Anniversary gathering had brought one the largest number of law enforcement personnel to New York City. There were over

3,000 police and Federal agents assigned to protect approximately 180 delegates from around the world. Every federal law enforcement bureau was involved with the central command at 1 Federal Plaza. That explained why the secret service agents would have wanted us to move the dinner to Manhattan where they would have felt more in control protecting President Castro.

xi    That 1985 campaign for Borough President was the first time that the Puerto Rican vote in the South Bronx came out in droves and almost equaled the concentrated Anglo vote of Co-Op City that had always been the strongest wide voting block in the borough.

xii   When I interviewed, now Senator, Reverend Ruben Diaz for this book he admitted that protestors were paid, but stated that he did not pay them. He stated that he facilitated the process for them to get paid. I also learned that he was not the only Puerto Rican elected official to be contacted by the Cuban American National Foundation. Apparently, both Senator Efrain Gonzalez and Assemblyman José Rivera had been contacted as well. I was able to speak to Senator Efrain Gonzalez and Assemblyman José Rivera refused to be interviewed.

xiii  That scene and picture of Julio Antonio standing with Fidel Castro raising his arm like a boxing champ with that glove appeared to be the media's favorite. That was seen on CNN and the picture appeared in a special historical, limited edition book published in Cuba: Cien Fotos De La Revolución Cubana (100 photographs of the Cuban Revolution). Of the millions of photographs taken of the Cuban revolution, a special committee of historians, sociologist, professors and members of the Cuban Central Committee picked only 100 to be published in this special book. That photograph was one of the 100 chosen, confirmation that the dinner in the Bronx was indeed a special dinner for President Fidel Castro and the Cuban people.

xiv During my research in Cuba I had the pleasure to meet and become friends with, Roberto Chile. Mr. Chile was Fidel's personal photographer for over 20 years and was gracious enough to supply me with the video tape recordings of the event. Thanks to him I was able to relive the entire event as he had much of the bits and pieces of the evenings event from the police escort through the streets of the South Bronx leading to the restaurant to President Castro's speech. Thanks to his documentation I was able to deliver to each of the ladies and some friends pictures of them present that evening.

xv President Castro received 230 invitations to breakfast, lunch, or dinner according to John Kavulich, President of the U.S. - Cuba Trade and Economic Council. (New York Times, Oct. 20th - Pg. A.7: "Visiting Castro To Meet Both Cold Shoulders & Fidelmania," By Lizette Alvarez

xvi I was not the only one affected by my involvement in the dinner for President Fidel Castro. In my interviews for this book when I spoke to Carlos Nazario, President of the National Puerto Rican Business Council he shared that as a result of his participation in the dinner he had long-time business associates that were in his same line of business that ended their friendship over his participation in the dinner with President Castro.

46088941R00138

Made in the USA
Middletown, DE
22 July 2017